Dedication

I dedicate this book to the outreach development workers: to their spirit and their conviction in defining sex and sexuality.

We owe our tomorrow to them, after all.

About the author

Madhu Bala Nath was born in New Delhi, India, in 1954. She studied History and Agrarian Economy at Delhi University and obtained an MA degree in 1975. She began her career as a free-lance researcher, working with grass-roots organisations concerned with women's issues.

After having worked with UNIFEM as the Regional Programme Advisor involved with the development and backstopping of UNIFEM programmes in India and South East Asia, she moved into the compelling and rather unexplored issue of HIV/AIDS, working as the regional adviser for the UN Development Programme's regional programme on HIV/AIDS for Asia and the Pacific. As the Gender and HIV Advisor to UNAIDS/UNIFEM based in New York since 1997, she has been responsible for undertaking programme implementation and advocacy with UN agencies, national governments and partners from civil society to enable the incorporation of gender concerns in HIV issues into their programmes.

In the course of her assignments she has always gained synergy by working at the grassroots. During her last assignment, she had a close association with men and women living with the HIV virus, and with communities which were very vulnerable to the epidemic. The writing of this book is an attempt to understand the toll the epidemic is taking, not just in terms of compiled statistics or through banal platitudes at national and international seminars, but through the subjective experiences of the people themselves and through the first-hand knowledge which the author has gained from working with them.

From Tragedy Towards Hope

Madhu Bala Nath

Commonwealth Secretariat
Marlborough House
Pall Mall
London SW1Y 5HX
United Kingdom

Printed in the United Kingdom by Formara Limited

The author has asserted her moral right to be identified as an author of this work.

Whenever possible, the Commonwealth Secretariat uses paper sourced
from sustainable forests or from sources that minimise a destructive impact
on the environment.

Copies of this publication can be ordered direct from
The Publications Unit
Commonwealth Secretariat
Marlborough House
Pall Mall
London SW1Y 5HX
United Kingdom
Tel +44 (0)20 7747 6342
Fax +44 (0)20 7839 9081
e-mail r.jones-parry@commonwealth.int

Price: £10.99   ISBN: 0-85092-676-9

Web sites:
http//www.thecommonwealth.org   http//www.youngcommonwealth.org

Contents

A tribute to
an unknown face . . . . .

As I entered a small square room in the Kenyan slum of Pumwani, I had my first encounter with pain and helplessness. A certain inadequacy enveloped me. I stood speechless as I saw a frail 30-year-old woman with a body that was obviously in pain. This was AIDS in its most painful manifestation. I wanted to reach out to her, to erase her wounds, but I could do next to nothing to lessen her suffering. And as I stood there without words, she reached out to me and said 'We all have to die. I have had AIDS for the past four years, but it has not deterred me, instead it taught me to see the finer things in life'.

Her memory remains, lingering, nagging guilt remains, and a deep-seated respect lies buried within me. It haunts me at every juncture, in shades that will never pale or fade away.

And as I put pen to paper I bow my head in obeisance, in guilt, in sorrow, in prayer for that unknown woman.

Acknowledgements

This book would not have been possible without the tremendous support provided to this area of work by Dr. Noeleen Heyzer, Executive Director of the United Nations Development Fund for Women (UNIFEM). Her commitment to improving the lives and livelihood of women across the globe provided the enabling space for this work to be completed.

Dr. Peter Piot, Executive Director, UNAIDS and Dr. Awa Marie Collseck, Director, Policy, Strategy and Research, UNAIDS have remained strong pillars of support. Their undying efforts to relentlessly respond to the issues of the HIV/AIDS epidemic generated the necessary motivation in me to move ahead even in times of despair and frustration.

The much-needed community-based empirical data that have lent substance to this work were generated in the UNIFEM field offices and I would like to take this opportunity to thank the UNIFEM Regional Teams – Chandni and Suneeta, Guadalupe and Eva, Gita and Martha, Aster and Charlotte, Joycelin and Dawn, and Mai Do and Madam Binh, for providing invaluable support for the community-based research that was conducted.

The support provided by the Commonwealth Secretariat to this effort remains invaluable as it has enabled us to reach out to our partners in a number of countries across the globe.

Ms Tracy Carvalho and Ms Lindsay Flury have provided administrative and logistical support in all the work that I have undertaken and I would like to acknowledge their assistance with gratitude and appreciation.

Vatsala has tirelessly edited the work in spite of burdening time schedules and Bharati has made the text come alive, giving a face to the words and life to the letters. Thank you, Vatsala and Bharati, for being there to enrich my efforts once again.

Finally, I wish to thank Kanwal, my husband, for encouraging me in every step that I took which led to my involvement with issues of gender and HIV/AIDS that culminated with this book. He restored my faith in humanity when I was losing it, and provided the courage I needed to understand and absorb the injustices, trials and tribulations that make human life different and yet so meaningful.

Madhu Bala Nath

Foreword

The toll of both the statistics and devastation that HIV/AIDS is taking around the world can leave us feeling hopeless and helpless. That is why this publication *"Voices from Tragedy to Hope"* can assist us all. It demonstrates the immense gains for everyone that can result from the force of human will and, in particular, the empowerment of those affected with HIV/AIDS when actively involved in solutions to fighting this pandemic. We are only beginning to recognize the huge gender issues within HIV/AIDS. By better understanding these forces, we can collectively begin to address the pandemic more effectively. This publication helps us in that quest.

The Commonwealth Secretariat has as one of its most important priorities the global fight against HIV/AIDS. We are honoured to work with the author, Madhu Bala Nath and the United Nations Fund for Women (UNIFEM) on the promotion of this publication that will help us all in this urgent quest.

Nancy Spence
Director, Gender and Youth Affairs Division

Introduction

The world of HIV/AIDS is riddled with complexities. In the industrialised world, the discovery of and reasonable access to powerful anti-retroviral drugs have caused death rates due to AIDS to plummet, and opened up newer and greener vistas for people living with HIV/AIDS. The same discovery for our partners living with HIV/AIDS in the developing countries has been rather agonising. 'It is like seeing food when you are starving but you cannot eat it.' The drugs are astronomically expensive. The Health Minister of Uganda recently explained to the global community in the United Nations Security Council that providing these drugs to Uganda's two million people living with HIV/AIDS would cost 12 times the nation's annual budget.

The fight over drugs called anti-retroviral has generated a lot of publicity. Pharmaceutical companies like Glaxo and Bristol-Myers Squibb are under fire by activists. Though the development of some of these drugs was funded through public money by some governments, the pharmaceutical companies are today arguing that since they purchased the patents from the governments and invested heavily in clinical trials, it is they who should rightly control the price of the drugs, and all the more so as the profits feed new research.

But as these controversies rage, men and women are coping with some basic structural lacunae as they live with HIV/AIDS. With hospitals running at 170 per cent of their capacity, they are limiting the stay of their patients to two days only. Poverty stricken patients are opting to be discharged as they near death because it is cheaper to transport a person when he/she is alive than it is to transport a dead body. A study in Zambia has recently pointed out that when a patient dies, the family mourns not only the loved one but also the end of food aid.

Men and women in large families living in crowded slums are struggling with the issues of minimum private space to be able to use a condom to have safe sex. Young girls have little or no option to guard their reproductive tracts from sexually transmitted diseases (STDs) with no water available to keep their genitals clean during menstruation. Malnourished and anaemic pregnant women are facing the risks of receiving a transfusion of unsafe blood every time they conceive, deliver or abort a baby. The concepts of patriarchy and masculinity remain entrenched in societies, and women and womanhood continue to be perceived as symbols of and providers of sexual gratification and emotional domination.

Development agencies have been working for decades on issues relating to poverty eradication; the concept of poverty has been redefined by the Human Development Report to include broader parameters of knowledge, longevity and access to basic resources. Issues of access to shelter, housing, water sanitation, food and education have been highlighted, critiqued and ostensibly addressed in global conferences. The international human rights instruments have been orchestrated, signed and ratified through intergovernmental processes. Yet, as newer challenges like that of HIV/AIDS appear on the horizon, these basic dilemmas of access and control; of equity and distribution; of power and power relations continue to plague the survival of men and women on this planet.

It is in this state of strange paradoxes that UNIFEM and UNAIDS have been trying to improvise ways and means to prevent the spread of the epidemic and minimise the negative effects on men and women. Arising out of a need expressed by the women's movement, UNIFEM has been a barometer for the emerging needs of women in various parts of the world. And as the HIV/AIDS epidemic matures, UNIFEM has been recording the impact of this emerging development challenge on women. In the early 1990s, the epidemic was compartmentalising women into 'good' and 'bad' because of a wave of anti-AIDS messages that portrayed women as vectors of the disease. By the mid-1990s, the virus was affecting the lives of the 'good' women – women who had had only one sexual partner in their entire lives.

Data from Mexico indicate that by the mid-1990s, only 0.8 per cent of all reported AIDS cases were among sex workers, but 9 per cent were among housewives. By December 1997, in Francistown, Botswana, 43 per cent of pregnant women were testing positive in a major surveillance exercise. During the same period, UNAIDS had declared that heterosexual intercourse was accounting for 70 per cent of all global adult infections.

For UNIFEM, the challenge was further exacerbated by the figures put out by the World Health Organization (WHO) on sexually transmitted diseases in 1995. Increase in STD cases indicated an increase in unsafe sex. WHO had estimated that in 1995 there were 333 million cases of STDs, of which 65 million were in sub-Saharan Africa and 150 million were in south and south-east Asia. The presence of STDs increases the risk of HIV transmission five-fold. With a macro scenario boding a blow to the wellbeing of men and women, the information from the field was equally disturbing.

In some villages of Uganda, focus group discussions revealed that not a single woman had seen a condom. A behavioural survey in Tamil Nadu in India showed that 82 per cent of the male STD patients had had sexual intercourse with multiple partners within the preceding 12 months and only 12 per cent had used a condom. Data from the same country revealed that 90 per cent of the male clients of male sex workers were married. In South Africa 71 per cent of the girls had experienced sex against their will.

3

With this as the backdrop, and in response to the needs of women, UNIFEM launched a pilot initiative entitled 'Gender Focussed Responses to Address the Challenges of HIV/AIDS'. Partnering this effort were the United Nations Population Fund and the United Nations Joint and Co-sponsored Programme on HIV/AIDS. The aim was to co-ordinate the women's movement in a number of countries, thereby strengthening and expanding the response to the epidemic. The violence campaign launched by UNIFEM during the fiftieth anniversary of the Universal Declaration of Human Rights in 1998 became the entry point to the effort. Kraus, Goldamt and Bula in their analysis entitled 'Partner Violence in Joint HIV and Substance Abuse' had highlighted that 96 per cent of the women living with HIV/AIDS had experienced violence. At the same time, information was forthcoming from Rwanda where the HIV/AIDS virus was being used as a weapon of war, ensuring that large numbers of women would die of sadness.

During the following 18 months, a series of workshops on gender, HIV and human rights was conducted in 9 countries over three geographical regions aimed at enhancing understanding of the gender dimensions of the epidemic. A number of community-based studies on gender and HIV/AIDS were commissioned to capture the voices of women infected and affected by the mutating virus, and to provide a safe and credible space for these women within decision-making processes at the national level.

Education and communication strategies on the epidemic were undertaken with a new spirit of understanding, based on real life situations rather than on value-loaded judgements on people's sexual behaviour. A spirit of inclusion involving those affected by the virus was fostered to reduce the stigma associated with the disease. Myths and rituals around sexuality were explored, visited, revisited and understood as the organisation adjusted its approaches from being a learning organisation before it could become a knowledge provider.

And as we explored and sought information, a key issue that kept arising was that if sexuality and gender, the two most insidious forms of oppression against women, were at the core of the epidemic, what could be done to reduce women's susceptibility to HIV/AIDS? How could men be engaged in efforts that would reduce these vulnerabilities? How could paradigms be transformed to capture new and emerging controversies?

The chapters that follow detail the mysteries that were unravelled in the area of human sexuality and its interface with gender relations and other power structures. The discussions also highlight the strengths and weaknesses of existing policy and programme frameworks that have been set up to respond to the challenges being posed by HIV/AIDS. Personal anecdotes, observations by real people, empirical data, both community-based and at the macro level, have been used to present the truth, the core issues of unfathomable tragedies and emerging hopes of men and women living with the virus – the virus that is causing AIDS.

Chapter One

Images of the Epidemic

Working on development issues for close to two decades is bound to leave its mark – it has. Images, stark, poignant, ridden at times with pathos, at times with courage, come to my mind as a visual collage:

❖ young, vulnerable pre-adolescents, victims of the HIV virus, confusion and bewilderment written large across their faces
❖ an HIV-infected man, refused treatment, lying in a subway ditch cleaning his own sores
❖ families going without food because the bread-winner is dying of HIV.

Images of people traumatised and victimised – shell-shocked victims of a mental and physical holocaust – have left me bewildered. Snatches of first-hand experiences of the epidemic nag at my consciousness and provide occasion for me to look more closely and examine in a harsh light all that has been done and remains to be done. It is against this backdrop that I share the tragedies and the triumphs, the myths and the realities, that have accompanied the virus . . .

On the shores of Lake Victoria, in the Kagera region of Tanzania, lives Protase Karani, who heads a home-based care team. He has seen the desolation and the despair that plagues the families of the victims. When a man sees his wife die of AIDS and his son or daughter returns from the city also sick, he looks straight at his own future where an early death will consume him too. He has little else to turn to except alcohol. His rationale seems faultless – why should he invest in the future? Why should he spend money on coffee trees that will take several years to mature, or plough more land than is necessary to feed his family this year? Today, many people are spending whatever money they have on liquor because they say 'What is the point? I shall die soon too . . . '

In Kasheni, a Tanzanian village bordering Lake Victoria, village chairman Gerald Ndyckobola turns the yellowed pages of a personal file. Among the portraits of family groups is a photo of 11 fit and smiling young men who made up the local football team. The photograph strikes him like a sledge-hammer. More than half the figures are now marked with an ink cross indicating the reach of the virus.

Feliciana's husband refused for months to believe he had AIDS, certain that he had been bewitched. He spent all his family's savings on futile visits to the witch doctor. When he finally recognised the nature of his illness, he sold off bits of his shambha (farmland) to buy medicines on the black market. He died soon, leaving a wife suffering from AIDS and six children. When Feliciana is fit enough, she labours on other people's farms, and when she is too ill to work, the family simply goes without food. They rise and retire with the sun, for Feliciana cannot afford even candles to light her tiny house after dark.

And, as the sun sets on this city (Lusaka), casting shadows over the modern government-sponsored high-rises, entire families, in contrast, settle for the night on the sidewalks. Scattered among them are the ragged street children, many of who make money as sex workers and look for any means to get high. Workers at the Fountain of Hope, a non-profit organisation that works with the street children, say that the children have even found a way of getting a powerful high from fermented human faeces, a substance known as jekem.

Ralph Hernandez lay on the hospital bed at the Addis Ababa Armed Forces Hospital dying a slow, agonising death. The only drug available in the hospital dispensary for his condition had elicited an allergic reaction. He had shed his skin and his body wept like a giant wound. His breathing was fast; shallow sunken eyes were closed. The nurses had no pain-killers on hand to ease his suffering. Ralph Hernandez had his story to tell. 'Once I went to a hospital in New York City. They asked me if I had Medicaid. When they found out I did not have Medicaid, they did not want to help me', said Ralph Hernandez. 'They did not even clean my sores, they just gave me antibiotics and put me out on the street to clean them myself. Now how am I going to keep my sores clean when I'm living in the subway ditch?' With anti-retroviral treatment 'my tongue falls asleep, I have a low body temperature, dizziness, headache and a hypersensitive skin'.

'I told my mother about it when I read a love letter which I found in my husband's pocket and realised that he was seeing other women. She asked me to have patience and go back to him, since that is how men behave. When I told my friends in the church, they asked me not to tell anyone since in view of my position there would be a scandal if people learnt that I had left my husband because he was flirting. They advised me to continue to stay with him and pray for him to change his behaviour. But here I am now, doomed forever . . . ,' the 35-year-old Christian preacher from Ghana and mother of three sons weeps as she tells her story.

Somehow I feel responsible for the tragedy I write about. The degree of apathy that we are capable of as people is sadly illustrative of the adage that the more things change the more they are the same. But change is not an overnight phenomenon.

My thoughts meander along like a winding river and I also see the brave faces. I can see snapshots of women standing upright, their voices ringing clear and bold.

In rural Haiti, poor women affected by the virus are telling the story of a woman living with HIV through a video presentation, using this as a means to educate the community. Proud of their success in being able to break the myths around the epidemic, the women have been speaking of their experiences at a number of meetings. In one of these meetings, a Haitian physician commented 'What kind of success is this? If we are failing to prevent HIV transmission in the region, what is the significance of your work?' The poor women did not hesitate and answered, 'Doctor, when all around you liars are the only cocks crowing, telling the truth is victory!'

In the state of Tamil Nadu in India, Sarita lives with the HIV virus. Her words linger in the air. 'Counselling helped through the initial shock and ensuing depression. Soon I knew I had won. The frustration gradually wore off. I am now filled with hope and strength to live my life to the fullest, even with HIV/AIDS. Nothing will keep me down. As a first step, I have divorced my husband. The next thing I have done is to take up a job. Financial independence has made my life meaningful even if it is destined to be short.'

Famous last words. Sarita's words and tragedy are not her story alone. It might be Jennifer, Zohra or Kamla. They survive through it all – the onslaughts of life and destiny. And rising above all, braving pain and bracing themselves against adversity, the women are once again proving their resilience and living positively, in demographics that are fast changing because of HIV/AIDS.

Chapter Two

Living Positively in Changing Demographics

A changing demography

The epidemic is taking its toll . . . According to the latest population report prepared by the population division of the UN Department of Economic and Social Affairs, children born in 29 sub-Saharan African nations face a life expectancy of just 47 years because of the toll the epidemic is taking in the region. This life expectancy figure represents a 16-year drop. In the absence of HIV/AIDS life expectancy in these countries would have been 63 years. What will the demographics look like?

Sparser population

In a recent study of the impact of HIV/AIDS on demography, conducted by the US Census Bureau in 23 countries, it has been stated that the most severe demographic effect of HIV/AIDS will be experienced by countries years after the epidemic has peaked. According to this report, life expectancy will drop to 40 years or less in 9 sub-Saharan African countries by 2010. According to the findings of the same study, AIDS will reduce population growth rates to less than half of their expected levels by 2010 and they may remain low or negative for many years. However, in most countries, population growth will remain positive because fertility rates will remain high, except in three countries, Botswana, Guyana and Zimbabwe, where fertility rates may drop sufficiently to result in a negative population growth by the year 2010.

Many orphaned children

A corollary to shorter life expectancies is the increase in the number of orphaned children. According to the analysis of the US Census Bureau, by the year 2010 the numbers of children who will have lost their mothers or both parents due to HIV/AIDS will swell to 22.9 million. As a result, in sub-Saharan Africa there will be 12 times as many children under 15 as adults over 64. With this as the backdrop, the images of the epidemic in Africa are of families which have a cognitive unfamiliarity. We are already looking at families headed by children. The ailing old surrounded by children little aware of how to tend the old and the sick; communities on the brink of survival trying to cope with the demands of productive labour; or sick women tending sick children. These are the conditions and projections today for the 23 million people living with AIDS in this region.

The impact in Asia is projected to be worse than in sub-Saharan Africa. Though HIV was a late comer to Asia and the Pacific, its spread has been swift. Since 1994, almost every country in the region has seen HIV prevalence rates increase by more than 100 per cent. Today, 6.4 million people in Asia are believed to be living with HIV. Considering that this region houses 60 per cent of the world's sexually active population, one can only apprehend with horror what might be the course of the epidemic in this region.

In Latin America, 1.3 million people are living with HIV. The distinguishing factors of the pattern of development in this region are a high external debt, an equally high debt service ratio, a low food production capacity and very high urbanisation. This has resulted in problems of development that increase poverty and give it a feminine face. For poverty that is urban is rootless, is characterised by the growth of a low productivity informal sector (where women cluster for subsistence) and by rapid demographic changes reflecting the disintegration of families and communities. A special feature of the epidemic in this region is the high number of young people who are at risk, especially street children forced out of the security of a stable household as a result of the fast urbanisation. A survey in Rio de Janeiro revealed that 60 per cent of young boys aged 15–19 engaged in sexual intercourse. Rates as high as this have not been seen in samples of male teenagers in other parts of the world.

In recent decades, north Africa and the western Asian region have witnessed major political, social, economic and demographic upheavals, which have led to the exacerbation of existing, fairly large, gender disparities. The persisting Gulf War and other armed conflicts like the Iran-Iraq war, the oil conflict between Iraq and Kuwait, and civil wars in Algeria and Somalia have created mass displacement of populations. UNAIDS estimates that the region has 210,000 HIV-positive people, 20 per cent of whom are women. The epidemic is, however, not even in its spread and these figures need to be seen as averages. UNAIDS estimates that 75 per cent of the region's reported cases relate principally to five countries: Morocco, Saudi Arabia, Sudan, Tunisia and Djibouti.

In Eastern Europe, though the absolute numbers are lower, many countries have experienced the doubling or tripling of infections since 1994. As the epidemic advances in a geometric progression, what is it doing to the lives of men and women?

Women bearing a quadruple burden

Today, approximately 46 per cent of the 33.6 million adults living with HIV/AIDS are women, and the proportion is growing. Of the 16,000 new infections occurring every day, the percentage of women infected is 50 per cent. Following a trend observed in other countries, male to female ratios among HIV-infected persons have begun to equalise. In Brazil, the ratio stood at 16:1 in 1986 but the figures for 1997 indicate the ratio as 3:1.

Women's susceptibility to the virus has gradually been increasing.

In a perverse twist, the epidemic has led to a further exploitation of children in many parts of the world. Estimates of the number of child prostitutes in Thailand range from an optimistic 100,000 to over 800,000. Fifty to 80 per cent of these children, it is estimated, are already infected.

The report on the global epidemic issued by UNAIDS in June 1998 reports a cumulative total of AIDS deaths in sub-Saharan Africa of 9.6 million, leaving behind 7.8 million orphans. South and south-east Asia record a cumulative total of 7.3 million deaths due to AIDS and a cumulative number of orphans of 200,000. If these numbers of AIDS orphans are juxtaposed with the rising numbers of women living with HIV, the crippling burden of care on women's lives and livelihoods becomes a glaring reality. We will keep witnessing shifts in the status of women and assaults on their dignity and rights unless we take cognisance of their multiple roles in society. Women have been bearing the triple burden of production, reproduction and management of the household resources. The HIV epidemic has created a situation, which has exacerbated this burden. Women today are carrying the quadruple burden of sheltering and caring for orphans.

The changing family system

'The extended family in Africa is far better than the West about taking in relatives', says Mark Louden. 'There is no formality about taking care of cousins. They slip right into saying mom. In Africa, you can have 30 moms. The problem is that AIDS just doesn't take one woman in a family. It tends to take all the wives of the brothers because the brothers tend to behave similarly.' The epidemic in Africa has confronted development workers with a dilemma – the dilemma of a silent breakdown of an informal social institution, the extended family. Will the extended family continue to act as a social security net for people affected by HIV/AIDS? Unfortunately, in some parts of Africa, it is already showing signs of nervous vulnerability.

'Edith and Khuzini Banda lived with their aunt for about a year after their mother died in 1994. But then the aunt said her home was too crowded. She sent the girls, then 13 and 14 years old, to live alone in their own house. The girls make do by renting out half of the two-roomed house for $15 a month and begging from their neighbours when food runs out.' The message from this state of affairs is clear.

The escalating costs of caring are increasing the demands on women's unpaid labour within the family. The economic costs of care in actual terms by way of medicines and treatment are also very high. In Kerala, in India, it has been estimated that the monthly costs incurred by the family for the treatment of opportunistic infections for an HIV-infected child is thrice the monthly income of the family. In Haiti, Marie Ange Viaud, 24 years old, was living with HIV and the cost of the ten medications prescribed for her was well in excess of $10,000 per year.

Female-headed households

How then will households cope? Community-based research has shown that the socio-economic impact of the epidemic on families has different repercussions depending on whether it is the man or the woman who dies. The epidemic is now at a stage of maturity in some countries of Africa where deaths as a result of AIDS are escalating, particularly among men. A significant finding of a study on the socio-economic impact of HIV on rural families in Uganda by Daphne Topouzis is that there are far more women who have lost their husbands to AIDS than men who have lost their wives. In Tororo, Helen Onyango of TASO reported that only 5 of her 62 clients were widowers. The rest were young widows from 15–35 years of age. The epidemic is therefore contributing directly to an increase in female-headed households.

Studies by the Food and Agriculture Organisation in Uganda and East Africa show that the main problem for many AIDS affected female-headed households is access to food and the consequent malnutrition.

'Jane, 23, has two children, four and two years old, and lives in Bumanda village in Tororo. Her husband, a farmer, died of AIDS. Both her children have been sick for a long time and she believes that they are also infected. Jane has not been able to work in the shambha for the last three months due to her husband's illness and the fact that the family has lost three other members in the last month. Her husband has been dead just a month and she is already experiencing food shortages. About once a week she prepares only one meal a day. The family diet consists of cassava and millet bread, occasionally eaten with smoked fish. She says she has no money to buy salt and cooking oil.

Another constraint is labour shortage and a negligible flow of cash income, which follows. According to Gabriel Rugalema, the most immediate need recorded by widows in Tanzania was credit to establish small projects that could combine farm and domestic work.

Women today are experiencing a sudden change in their roles in agricultural production. They are finding themselves lacking in the requisite skills and experience to respond effectively to the new challenges that confront them in their new roles. In Zimbabwe, women are having to move into industries that were previously dominated by men, for example carpentry, with little or no resources to cope with this shift. A direct consequence is a sudden decline in productivity. This is, in fact, the female face that poverty is acquiring in countries affected with HIV/AIDS. This feminisation of poverty is different from earlier trends. This poverty is often new for some households, and there is a potential danger of it becoming intergenerational and deep-rooted.

Exacerbating poverty

Studies have shown that the impact of HIV/AIDS on a specific demographic group depends on that group's awareness about the disease and the way it is transmitted, and the susceptibility or vulnerability of the group to high-risk situations. Studies investigating these issues were supported by the UN Development Programme/Asian Development Bank in India and Sri Lanka. The studies found a strong positive correlation between education (with a component of sex education) and income levels, and awareness about HIV/AIDS. In short, the evidence from these studies suggests that, at least anecdotally, the disadvantaged will be disproportionately affected by the epidemic. Women all over the developing world form a large majority of this group.

Research on the impact of HIV/AIDS on the household is being undertaken in a number of countries but few studies have examined gender as a variable in measuring the household and community impact of the epidemic. The little that has been explored has come up with the following findings:

❖ In communities where women are responsible for subsistence farming, when they become infected the cultivation of subsistence crops falls, resulting in an overall reduction in food availability in the household;

❖ When opportunistic infections begin to occur, in the absence of access to medicines, sickness is prolonged and girls are often pulled out of school before boys to fulfil household duties when help cannot be hired due to the depletion of household economic resources;

❖ As a result of the loss of income from a male income earner when he falls ill, women and children are required to seek other sources of income. Research has shown that adolescent girls may be particularly vulnerable as a result of bartering sex for cash or other resources.

Other evidence suggests that the epidemic is contributing to a downward trend in the age of marriage for young women, as men seek younger wives to protect themselves from infection and families seek the economic protection of marrying off their daughters to economically stable men. This phenomenon has far-reaching consequences in terms of access to education by young girls, diminished access to productive resources, economic dependency on the male partner and poor reproductive health as a result of early intercourse and childbearing.

In instances where the male head of household has died, studies have shown how women face a tragic set of circumstances in terms of loss of social support from family members, ostracism from the community and lack of legal protection of their right to inherit land and property. Instances have been cited where a husband's family may blame a widow for the death of her husband and refuse to accept her or her children into the family support system. Other instances have been cited where family members encourage a husband who is asymptomatically HIV-positive to leave his wife who is also infected and find another woman.

Reprioritising national spending

There is thus a potentially important synergy between AIDS mitigation and anti-poverty programmes, especially those anti-poverty programmes that are gender sensitive. Rural development programmes aimed at improving women's access to sustainable livelihoods are likely to lessen the impact of the epidemic. For example, access to clean water is likely to have a marked effect on the amount of time women have for other productive activities and for the care of the sick and orphans. Access to labour saving technologies such as fuel-efficient stoves and food-grinding machines will similarly increase the amount of time women have to be able to shoulder new burdens.

The World Bank finding that each adult death depresses per capita food consumption in the poorest households by 15 per cent, implies that in responding to the epidemic, national governments will need to use adult death and household dependency ratios as a targeting criteria for poverty alleviation programmes. And as we reprioritise our national spending, we will need to do it even more critically with a gender lens. Women in Asia living with the virus are today silently expressing a need for support to break abusive relationships.

They need support for their children to be placed in foster homes, access to housing, hospices and, above all, access to a stable means of livelihood.

Living positively

Women living with HIV today are challenging existing norms around sexuality. There is a firmness and conviction in the statements being made. Says Lydia, who for eight months weathered bouts of diarrhoea, fought herpes zoster, lived with a horrible persistent cough, vomited most of what she ate and bore drenching night sweats and ulcers:

> The Kenyans should stop cheating themselves about this disease. Let us stop pretending about the problem. The problem is real. I am a living example. There are thousands suffering out there. The disease is spreading like wildfire every day and night. So why all this pretence? Many people are engaging in promiscuous behaviour as if there is no AIDS. AIDS is here with us. The sooner we face the reality as individuals and as a society the better for us all.

In Uganda, Agnes, living with HIV, is successfully resisting wife inheritance. 'Poverty is not an excuse for wife inheritance', she says. She thinks that women can resist being inherited but such self-assertiveness largely depends on how they are raised and on the type of relationship they had with their husbands.

Patricia, in Tororo village, is working towards setting up a group in her village to encourage girls to develop life skills so that myths around sexuality can be exploded and create income-generating opportunities that would keep them away from bad company, as she put it.

But the voices of Lydia or Patricia or Agnes, though firm, are not yet loud enough to close the yawning gap between people's beliefs, which have been imbibed over a long process of socialisation, and the appropriate sexual behaviour that is essential to stop the spread of HIV/AIDS. Each year thousands of men fall into this gap and thousands of women are dragged in with them. Because of gender socialisation processes, the need to prove themselves masculine propels men towards risky behaviour. Abstinence is seen as unnatural and refusal to use condoms is rationalised in many ways: 'It is only really sex when you ejaculate into a woman', says a Zimbabwean man; '"*real* men" do not get sick', says a Brazilian adolescent. Mexican sociologists Jose Aguilar and Luis Botello point out that condoms represent safety and are therefore unmasculine. And as more and more men conform to these stereotypes, women's susceptibility to the epidemic continues to increase.

Chapter Three

Myths and Rituals – Increasing Women's Susceptibility

New revelations

The initial years of my work gave me a rare insight into another form of women's exploitation through myths and rituals. Each myth and ritual that I came across confirmed my belief that, at times, the more things change the more they remain the same. In the present context they are indicative of the way in which women are susceptible to the HIV virus at every stage of their lives. An in-depth study of sex and sexuality across borders revealed a common strain, basic to the core issue of the entire exercise, that stood out like a stark fact. We worship goddesses – but shorn of the divine aura the flesh and blood woman has no status. Even when the occasional goddess is dragged to a human level, she suffers the fate of the ordinary lesser mortal woman. In Indian mythology even 'Sita', the revered goddess, went through baptism by fire to prove her chastity.

Interviews with various sections of the population, be it with representatives of non-governmental organisations, women in the slums, people living with HIV/AIDS, invariably left me humbled. How little I knew about sex and sexuality. This feeling kept nagging at me at every discussion, every personal interview, every anecdotal piece of evidence relating to the existing myths and rituals around sexuality. Country after country, whether in Asia, Africa or Latin America, had new revelations to offer.

❖ In China, I heard the myth that ground rhino horn increases male sexual virility.

❖ In India and Indo China, it is believed that having sex with a virgin is a cure for sexually transmitted diseases in men.

❖ Western Kenya abounds with stories from teenage peers that failure to indulge in sex results in back aches.

❖ The truckers in South Asia have been socialised to believe that it is important to release the heat generated in the body as a result of driving long distances sitting in hot cabins by having sex every 400 miles of driving.

❖ In Papua New Guinea, a widely prevalent prophylaxis for STDs is to cut the penis and drain off the possibly infected blood after an intercourse which could have been unsafe.

❖ In Mexico, it is officially acceptable for men to have sex with men, provided they take the active insertive role in anal intercourse as this is regarded as macho or super masculine.

❖ In many parts of Africa, women insert external agents into their vagina, including scouring powders and stones, to dry their vaginal passages because of the belief that increased friction is sexually more satisfying to the males and this will prevent them from 'wandering out'.

In South Asia, some cultures celebrate the girl's coming of age. Menarche is viewed as a symbol of the girl's fecundity and the family begins to think of arranging the girl's marriage. Among the rituals performed is a ceremonial bath and the distribution of sweets in the neighbourhood. However, linking menstruation to child bearing and de-linking it from sexuality is a mechanism by which the latent sexuality of a woman is curbed. Marriage soon after menarche is one method by which parents channel the potent sexuality of young women into a socially acceptable state – the state of a nurturing mother rather than a seductress. There is thus an enormous gap between women's lived experience and what women want sexual relations to be. Women in large parts of South Asia have sex, performing it as a duty, to attain a socially secure position or in order to become pregnant.

As soon as the young girl child gets pregnant the ritual of 'Vallaikappu' is performed. The hands of the pregnant woman are decked with bangles, ostensibly to deter any further conjugal relationships during the pregnancy period, and the completion of this ritual signals a temporary separation between the husband and the wife until the delivery and, in fact, until a few months after. It is during these periods of forced separation that men seek sexual gratification outside of marriage. The behaviour is more often than not condoned by society. The girl child, a young mother, returns to her husband's house once again to perform sex as a duty, little aware of her husband's infidelity and her own vulnerability to the epidemic.

In West Africa, a system of societal beliefs has been developed over time to manage the process of procreation. In the scale of social values, childbearing is elevated to a value which confers a high social status. On the other hand, a stigma is attached to a childless woman. In parts of West Africa, the ultimate punishment is reserved for barren women. They are denied formal funeral rights and are buried secretly at night outside the village. Thus, if a woman did have sex with a condom to protect herself from HIV/AIDS, how would she be able to prove that she is fertile? In fact, women in Nigeria practice painful practices to ensure fertility. In Nigeria, 'gishiri', or salt cut, is practiced traditionally. This involves an incision on the interior of the vagina as a cure for infertility.

The loss of life of a woman in childbirth is expressed as the falling of a soldier in the line of duty. Women, in a manner, have internalised this ethic of nobility and duty so that pain and discomfort emanating from

27

their sexual and reproductive roles are accepted as the very essence of womanhood. The psychological preparation of young girls for childbirth, instead of giving factual information on safe motherhood, aims to increase the threshold of the tolerance to pain. A common example is the advice given to young mothers to endure a level of effort equal to that which would be required to produce water by pressing hard enough on a stone. Because of this stoicism, vital life-threatening signals are not communicated until too late. Severe haemorrhage is viewed by women to be a good sign because the body is seen to be eliminating bad blood. The consequence is a poor state of reproductive health with lesions and cuts in the woman's reproductive tract. This, coupled with a societally induced inability to practice safe sex, has increased women's susceptibility to the epidemic.

In a UN Development Programme study paper entitled 'The socio-economic impact of HIV and AIDS on rural families in Uganda' the author, Daphne Topouzis, brings out the stark realities of such situations through the real story of Miriam. Miriam, a widow from Gulu, lost her husband to AIDS and is herself sick with AIDS. Soon after her husband's death, her brother-in-law tried to inherit her but she categorically refused so as not to infect him and his wife. He harassed her for almost a year and when she still held firm he cut off all financial support to her and her four children. Now he is trying to claim the land that his brother left. A widow's dilemma is whether to be inherited or be abandoned. Wife inheritance thus greatly facilitates the spread of HIV and has the potential of infecting several families very rapidly. When widows are inherited by their late husband's brother, they risk infecting them as well as their co-wives. If any of the wives deliver children, they may also be infected with HIV. In some cases, widows whose husbands have died of causes unrelated to the epidemic may become infected with HIV if the brother-in-law is already infected.

The story of Mariah gives an insight into the lived experience of HIV-positive women.

My name is Mariah and I come from rural Mutoko in Mashonaland East province. I am 35-years-old and have three children of 12, 8 and 5 years of age. I first knew of my HIV status when my husband got ill. We both went for an HIV test and we were counselled and given our results. We were both found to be HIV-positive. We decided not to tell anyone for fear of stigmatisation and ostracisation. We didn't even tell our three children because we felt that it would be very stressful and they might fail to understand what we were going through. My husband got worse and finally died late last year. His relatives insisted that I should be inherited by one of his brothers. This is when I decided to tell them that I was HIV-positive and that my husband had died of AIDS. My in-laws started accusing me of having killed their son and I was told to leave the family. I was also told that the children belonged to the man and so I was not to take the children with me. My in-laws even threatened that they would demand the bride price from my parents. I left my in-laws residence with nothing of my own. I went to stay with my aunt who introduced me to her friend who is also HIV-positive. I soon got to know about a local AIDS support group. I joined the group and have not regretted doing so since then. The group has advised me on how to get back my property and custody of my children.

Mariah had acted with courage, defying existing myths and rituals in a world where reality would otherwise have written on her tombstone, 'She died after passing her HIV to her husband. . . .' The rituals cited above are only indicative and not exhaustive. They are indicative of the way in which women are susceptible to the virus at every stage of their lifecycle – as young girls, as mothers, as wives and as widows.

The list of these myths and practices that have enshrouded human sexuality is long. In many cultures, the genitals are surrounded by mystery because they are the 'instruments' used to put curses on others. Among the Kikuyu, for example, the worst curse is that when a woman, the age of the person who is being cursed's mother, lifts her skirts and turns around.

The initial years of my work on the epidemic were replete with wonder and amazement, which at times often reached a level of shock.

I learnt through the women in Senegal who had been socialised to be submissive in sexual relations to their partners, for 'a woman who says "No" to her husband for sex will not have good children'. The mother's behaviour during the sex act is decisive for the future of the child.

I came across another myth around a sexual ritual related to female circumcision. Folklore had it that an uncircumcised woman is not satisfied by only one man. Thus non-circumcision may drive women to unfaithfulness. In the opinion of Senegalese men, therefore, female circumcision was a good thing since it 'rationalises women's desire and helps women resist men'. The custom was also considered a purifying act, as an uncircumcised woman was considered impure. The respondents in the study in Senegal unanimously agreed that gum tattooing (which was making women vulnerable to the epidemic) was really a good practice as it 'cleared the sight and let out bad blood and also reduced headaches'. Women in Senegal chose to indulge in this practice as it was considered that this increased the contrast between the gums and the teeth, thereby enhancing their beauty.

A culture of silence

The social construction of sexuality, with its inherent myths and values around morality, fertility and sexuality, has been used to project social values and norms that have been different for men and for women. Thus multiple sexual partnerships are accepted and condoned for men in many societies, whereas modesty and virginity as a value is central to the image of womanhood. Cultures in many parts of the world consider female ignorance of sexual matters a sign of purity and, conversely, knowledge of sexual matters and reproductive physiology a sign of easy virtue. Added to this is the absence of a positive language for sexuality. The existing language around sexuality is perhaps the most difficult means of articulating the same. A conspiracy of silence therefore continues to surround HIV/AIDS.

Women have found it difficult to overcome these barriers and have not been able to open up communication with clinicians and counsellors or even with their peers. Because women have been constrained in talking about sexuality, there is little known about the disease in women. Until now, men have formed the vast majority of subjects in studies that form the foundation for our current treatment of HIV infection with anti-retroviral therapy and our best knowledge about prophylaxis and treatment of opportunistic infections. Cotton and co-workers reviewed data regarding accrual of patients to multi-centre trials and found that only 6.7 per cent of the participants were women. As a result, timely diagnosis for women has been compromised by inappropriate case definitions of the symptoms for AIDS.

The existence and persistence of this social construction of sexuality has led to the evolution of a number of rituals that have made women more vulnerable to the epidemic. The rituals have varied forms in various countries. The underlying message that all these rituals portray is that women's sexuality represents the interface between two most potent and insidious forms of oppression that prevail in society – gender and sexuality. The reluctance to address these issues has limited the effectiveness of programmes designed to improve women's health, develop life skills and prevent HIV and other sexually transmitted diseases.

With such an entrenched knowledge base, how then can messages on safer sexual practices to prevent HIV/AIDS make an impact on the human mind – an impact that can foster a process towards positive behaviour change? In Zimbabwe, data obtained through community-based research carried out by women's organisations have strengthened, or rather complicated, these dilemmas even more. Researchers in Zimbabwe are recording how even today, in some parts of Matebeleland, the engagement of fathers-in-law with their daughters-in-law is a culturally sanctioned practice. As it is, women in the developing world marry men who are much older than them, have had a number of sexual encounters and are therefore epidemiologically more vulnerable to HIV/AIDS. What would be her level of vulnerability if culturally she is required to have sex with her father-in-law as well?

Myths are also rooted in the nature of denial that is associated with HIV/AIDS. Because HIV/AIDS is so frightening, there is a temptation to deny the existence of the disease. After all, wouldn't it be nice if the disease was not there? In large parts of the world, even today, there is a tendency to attribute HIV/AIDS to witchcraft, or to believe that a cure for the virus is available in traditional and alternative medicine. This precondition of the human mind has been keeping people from owning responsibility for their sexual decisions.

As I write, my mind meanders back to the cornerstone in the entire saga – the first myth surrounding women and HIV. AIDS was first detected as a distinct clinical syndrome in the summer of 1981, when physicians in California and New York noted clustering of unusual infections and cancers in their patients. Almost all these patients were young gay men, a group not previously known to have such 'opportunistic' infections. In August, a mere two months after the first cases were reported in men, the same syndrome was identified in a woman. It was soon apparent that women were also vulnerable and within a year or two there were data to suggest that women were as likely to become infected with the virus as men. The initial misunderstanding that AIDS was a disease of men could be attributed perhaps to a historical accident. Yet myths around the virus prevailed. In 1985, a cover story in *Discover*, a popular science magazine, dismissed the idea of a major epidemic in women. The explanation given was that because the rugged vagina was designed for the 'wear and tear of intercourse and birthing', it was unlikely that women would ever be infected in large numbers through heterosexual intercourse. Nevertheless, even as such projections were being written, HIV was affecting millions of women. By 1991, AIDS was a leading killer of young women in most large US cities. The first myth that women were not vulnerable or susceptible to the epidemic had been broken.

And yet the political will to confront reality was not forthcoming. I was attending a high level meeting of donors and the Government of India, attended by senior Secretaries of State, decision-makers from the donor community, and health experts and professionals. We were honoured to have the opportunity to hear the renowned epidemiologist, the famous Dr. James Chin, speak on the latest projections of the epidemic for India. His prognosis was alarming – a startling figure of 5 million Indians to be infected with HIV by the turn of the century. This figure surpassed the projections made for other diseases like tuberculosis and malaria which till then were considered more serious than HIV/AIDS. Whereas tuberculosis was affecting one in every 7 Indians, HIV was affecting one in every 120 Indians! What Dr. Chin was projecting seemed so unreal to our policy makers.

The meeting concluded with an unfortunate outburst. The Health Secretary admonished the revered epidemiologist – 'Dr. Chin, you are acting rather irresponsibly! This is just going to cause a scare in the Indian population! After all we Indians are not as promiscuous as the people in the other countries where the epidemic is raging. Do you understand our culture? How accurate are your projections? We need to look at the methodology used to arrive at these figures. To me they seem rather inflated.' My jaw dropped. I could visualise and feel the emerging challenge – the challenge of facing and overcoming the syndrome of complete denial caused by a sense of frustration, hopelessness and fear.

This psyche could be felt, seen and heard across the spectrum of our development partners. A year later I visited some highway interventions undertaken by some NGOs in India with the truck drivers. I was intrigued to see that the condoms were being used to repair the radiator leakages in the trucks. Discussions with the truck drivers and the cleaners revealed that the impact of the awareness campaigns on the use of the condoms as a preventive measure had been minimal. A very logical argument was offered by the truckers. 'Our fathers and forefathers were all truck drivers. They were not infected by HIV/AIDS. In fact they like us did have sex every 400 kilometres of driving as it was believed that this prevented accidents by letting the heat out of the body at regular intervals.'

Learning through unlearning

These discussions were signalling a message for our work. There could be no real success as far as imparting information about HIV/AIDS was concerned unless the old learning which had been entrenched in the human mind was somehow unlearned. It was with this task in mind that we set out to explore the myths and rituals surrounding sexuality.

What was really interesting was that the data were clearly revealing that there was no difference between the literate and the illiterate women in Senegal as far as knowledge about their bodies and their sexuality was concerned. Education with a well thought out component on the gender construction of sexuality was therefore needed to prevent the spread of HIV/AIDS in a country where myths and rituals are more deeply embedded in the human mind than bookish knowledge. The task is huge – where does one begin? The first step remains to be taken, and that is to document the existing myths and practices in each country and encourage a critique on the validity and use of such rituals within the contextual realities of the HIV/AIDS epidemic.

The process will not be an easy one. Questioning deep-rooted myths and rituals will invite anger, denial, frustration, even apathy, but if done with the spirit of inclusion and involvement of those whose power is at stake, at least a new social enquiry will begin. This enquiry will in turn raise questions, some which may not have answers today, but the process will uncover new vistas, new answers, on the path of discoveries, new solutions to fresh challenges and perhaps to the one challenge looming ahead of us – of combating the HIV/ AIDS virus.

Chapter Four

No Answers – Just Discoveries

The discovery

Phoenix-like, he rose from the ashes to resurrect himself. Everybody's whipping boy suddenly refused to be persecuted any more and fought hard and successfully to regain his credibility as a person. This is not a story on celluloid but a true story of a boy born in the alley of a red light area in Kalighat. This is the story of Mrinal Kanti Dutta.

Mrinal Kanti Dutta today spearheads a movement for sex workers' rights in the city of Calcutta in India. Mrinal was born in the alley of the red light area in Kalighat – an illegitimate child of possibly an honourable citizen of the country. To shelter him from the wrath of the locals, his mother sent him to a school in an adjacent locality. But as it turned out, Mrinal found himself belonging nowhere. His education had separated him from the offspring of other sex workers but his identity kept him ostracised from the social mainstream. The potential that was created as a result of this strange 'mix' was recognised by the All India Institute of Hygiene and Public Health, as it launched the STD/HIV Intervention project (SHIP) in the city. The SHIP, widely known as the Sonagachi project, started in 1992, experimenting in the area of public health to control the transmission of STD/HIV among the sex worker communities in Calcutta. During the course of the project, the focus broadened considerably beyond disease control to address the structural issues of gender, class and sexuality. The project used three fundamental principles: Respect, Recognition and Reliance. The belief that sex workers can best work for themselves had refined their strategies. In fact, from the time he took over, Mrinal Kanti Dutta introduced a fundamental change in the organisation, i.e. the inclusion of sex workers in the key managerial positions of the project. Today, 25 per cent of the positions have been reserved for sex workers. 'Only if there is no alternative will outsiders be considered', he says. This approach in fact comes from the ideological base of the project. This ideological base questioned cultural stereotypes, social denial and human marginalisation in a manner that is democratic, not authoritarian, a manner which was not confrontational and yet challenges power structures, working through them and with them so as to strengthen them as partners. The issue of HIV/AIDS was used as the entry point for this social transformation. The project invited members of the sex workers' community to act as motivators and peer educators and Mrinal was the first to join. As time progressed, the STD/HIV Intervention Project gradually developed into a full-fledged movement for sex workers' rights. Today, a union of sex workers called the Durbar Mahila Samanvaya Committee (DMSC) has been formed and the so called 'fallen women', or street walkers, have graduated to becoming vociferous advocates of legislation and recognition of their work as a profession.

Starting as a helper in the STD clinic, Mrinal went from strength to strength as this movement developed and finally became the head of the entire project. Interestingly this happened on the same day that the first major political victory for the organisation was won. The first victory came on May Day in 1999, as the state government recognised the self-regulatory boards set up by the sex workers with members from the state government's Social Welfare Department and the state Women's Commission. The history of this victory is in fact a unique story.

Sonagachi

For 400 years Sonagachi had been known as the area where vice and crime prevailed. Young virgins were brought and sold; sex was bought, mostly with some kind of coercion; legendary dons like Biswanath Bhattacharya sent tingles of fear up women's spines as they approached a brothel owner and shouted, 'We will take a girl from your house along with two bottles of beer or else . . . '. In this area of vice and crime also lived Ansar Ali who everybody knew had 15 wives and yet remained free to terrorise other girls in the area. This was the piece of land, Sonagachi, where Shankari Pal reminisces sadly, 'We got only slaps. Shoes were thrown at us, cigarette butts were stubbed on our cheeks.' People from 'respectable' society came to Sonagachi but under stress, taking pains to avoid any kind of recognition. Interestingly Sonagachi was the land that laid bare human power relations and resultant exploitations in the crudest form possible. It was here that the most vulnerable of the girls rose over a course of time to become exploitative and distasteful power brokers in the form of brothel owners or 'malkins'. They shrewdly negotiated the sale of flesh in the midst of an environment loaded with risk and violence. To put it in another way, Sonagachi was a land of negotiations – where agreements were being negotiated day in and day out. It was perhaps this skill in negotiation that was used effectively by the SHIP project to transform and reform the balance of power relations in the two most insidious areas of oppression for women, gender and sexuality.

Negotiations with the self

The first sex worker tested positive in Calcutta in Kidderpore in 1982. Subsequently, other cases were detected in the adjoining red light areas of Chetla, Bow Bazar, Sonagachi, Rambagan, Sethbagan, etc. As prevalence rates rose to 5 per cent, the World Health Organization moved the focus of its interventions to condom distribution through peer motivators. The respect and recognition provided by the project to 65 peer motivators/

educators transformed the lives of the sex workers. They acquired information and knowledge along with the green coats and staff identity cards, which rocketed their esteem 'both self and societal'. The transformation, however, was a result of a well thought out and transparently executed process. A series of activities was organised with the aim of promoting self-reliance, confidence and social dignity.

From the very beginning, the project made it very clear to the sex workers that in no way would the rehabilitation approach be adopted. The project had not been established as a 'saviour' of fallen women.

The project provided the peer educators with every semblance of paid employment, e.g. uniform, identity cards, attendance registers that gave them social recognition. Writes Madhabi Jaiswal, 'The project has enabled me to face society with confidence' and Pushpa adds, 'This apron has changed my life, my identity, now I can tell others that I am a social worker, a health worker'.

A series of discussions was conducted in an open environment which raised critical posers for the sex workers, 'Why am I where I am?'. Answers to these posers were provided not by anecdotal rationale but by empirical evidence. A base line survey conducted by the project, using a participatory methodology, recorded that penury and deprivation, both social and economic, were the main factors that drove women into the sex trade. 84.4 per cent of the sex workers were found to be illiterate. Only 8.6 per cent of the sex workers had come willingly to the sex trade; the rest were there because of acute poverty, a family dispute or because they had been misguided and kidnapped.

And as the women saw their vulnerability receiving the support of a structural framework, they moved away from perceiving themselves as 'sinners and loose women'. Today Reba Mitra, a peer educator, emphatically demands that the sex trade be recognised. 'You see in the society, people are engaged in various forms of employment. For us this trade is also an employment. Why wouldn't the government recognise it? Who says we are loose women?' Wonders Gita, 'Are we alone to blame? What about the men who come to us? Are they not also polluting the society?'. This awakening was a very significant transformation that the project had achieved. The sex workers of Calcutta had begun to challenge the age-old notions and were trying to reconstruct their identity. This was the first stage of negotiations towards safer sexual practices – a negotiation with the self.

Negotiations with the peers

Ironical as it may seem, as women in the sex trade were revisiting their own stereotypes and getting empowered in the process, an incident which precipitated their vulnerability occurred in the project area. In early September 1994, an NGO, with the help of the state government and the local police, forcibly collected blood samples from about 50 sex workers. Earlier they had dragged out a brothel owner to the local police station and threatened her with serious consequences if she did not co-operate with them in these research trials. It was at this juncture that the project saw that the empowerment of 65 peer educators, although a good beginning, still left large numbers of sex workers quite vulnerable. How would safer sex practices get entrenched with this as the backdrop? At the same time, this incident served as an eye opener to the peer educators who now began to view the whole issue within a framework of human rights. They began to feel that it was critical that an organised body of sex workers be set up to collectively fight such instances of assaults on their dignity and rights. The process of empowerment thus moved into the next stage of negotiations, from negotiations with the self to negotiations with the peers.

The ideology during this second level of negotiations remained consistent – the belief that sex work was an occupation and not a moral condition. And because sex work was an occupation, occupational hazards had to be identified and overcome. The occupational hazards were

STDs/HIV, violence and sexual exploitation. Unless these were overcome the whole struggle of getting the sex trade acknowledged as a profession would remain futile. With this as the rationale, the peer educators moved from house to house in the red light areas equipped with accurate information on how to prevent STDs/HIV, how to access medical care and how to question power structures that promoted violence. The fieldwork began at 10 a.m. and continued until 1.00 p.m. Each group of peer educators (four in each group) contacted 40–50 sex workers and 10–15 brothel owners daily. They encouraged the sex workers to attend the clinic for regular health check ups; they used flip charts and leaflets for effective dissemination of information on STDs/HIV; they carried condoms with them to distribute to the sex workers. As the project progressed they monitored the use of the condoms by giving cardboard boxes to the sex workers for disposal of the used condoms. When asked about the rate of condom use and whether it had shown signs of progress, Kamala Mukherjee and Isika Basu reply 'Look at the dustbins in the area and you will get the answer. The cardboard boxes are there to show that the rate of condom use has definitely gone up.' And as these activities promoted interaction amongst the community the approach of the project expanded. The project had begun as a targeted intervention to prevent the spread of HIV/AIDS, using the basic construct of a behaviour change strategy. But soon the main obstacles facing the successful implementation of the project were recognised as being socio-historical and not just behavioural. The social construction of sexuality, the lack of a social acceptance of sex work, legal ambiguities surrounding laws relating to sex work, were now recognised by the community as elements to be confronted, battled against and overcome.

This analysis became the anchor which enabled negotiation amongst the peers and brought them together to form the Durbar Mahila Samanvaya Committee. At that point, a leading daily, the *Ananda Bazar Patrika*, hailed this move with the headline, 'Sex workers form their own organisation'. The move was hailed because it was radically different from earlier attempts in this direction. The earlier attempts at bringing sex workers together had named themselves as fallen women's organisations, e.g. Patita Udhar Samiti. These attempts disallowed new notions of self and only served to enhance guilt and shame amongst their members. Abha Bhaiya has very aptly remarked, 'Such attempts have been apologetic rather than liberating', and have remained in the periphery, away from the mainstream women's movements.

Some critical and strategic approaches were used by the project towards enabling women to empower themselves through a process of negotiations with their peers. These included:

❖ Building on the historical but latent vibrancy in the sex workers community. As early as 1980, years before the project had begun, Asha Sadhukan, together with Putul Singh, Pramila Singh, Manju Biswas and some others, had formed Mahila Sangha. Braving threats, they carried on a sustained campaign against 'Langra', a local don who extorted money from the sex workers and they finally drove the notorious hoodlum away from the area. The peer educators used this success to stir emotions and rally people towards a common objective. This coming together had a direct bearing on promoting safer sexual practices. The clients soon found that at least in some clusters they could not move from one brothel to another in search of condom-free sex. The conditions were the same in all the brothels.

❖ Making sincere efforts to respond to the perceived needs of the sex worker community as and when they arose. For example, though the emphasis of SHIP was to oversee the sexual health needs of the sex workers, it made arrangements to provide non-formal education to the sex workers as and when the demand for literacy programmes arose. Vocational training programmes were conducted for aged sex workers in 1996–97 to respond to the demand for security in old age. The Usha

Multipurpose Society was set up as a credit and savings society and this helped former sex workers with self-employment schemes and the community at large to be liberated from the exorbitant rates of interest that the moneylenders demanded. More and more women joined as they found the process meeting their needs.

❖ Creating space for expression through the cultural platform of 'Komal Gandhar'. Komal Gandhar is a cultural theatre group formed by the sex workers themselves. This medium expanded the canvas of communication within which negotiating safe sex had a critical niche. It enabled the sex workers to come together to negotiate jointly with the clients, the pimps, the malkins and the police, in an environment that was non-threatening. 'It has given us the space to say things that reside in our hearts.' 'This medium has been very effective in setting a code of health conduct for our clients.'

❖ Working against patriarchy, not against men. The peer educators conducted a client survey as early as 1993. The survey revealed that only 51.5 per cent of the clients had heard of HIV/AIDS but even this group lacked awareness regarding the use of condoms. Regular use of condoms was found in 1.5 per cent of these clients and 72.7 per cent had never used a condom. A meeting with these clients or 'babus' was organised by the project to build alliances to promote safer sexual practice. About 300 clients attended. The discussions that began at this meeting led to the opening of evening clinics for the clients, where they could receive free treatment, counselling and access to condoms. Socio-cultural programmes were organised to introduce safer sex and HIV/AIDS messages targeting the clients. Today the clients have come together in a support group called the 'Sathi Sangha'. This group supports the sex workers in motivating new clients to use the condoms and the clients group provides support to the sex workers in their efforts to eliminate sexual violence in the area. It is interesting to note here, that a section of clients, or 'babus', had all along played a very significant role in the history of prostitution in Calcutta. During the days of the national movement in the early twentieth century, they inspired the Sonagachi women to raise funds to aid the freedom struggle.

Negotiating for safety with structures

The pimps

Things were never smooth sailing in Sonagachi. There has always been an undercurrent of control by vested interests, the police, the criminal and political nexus. 'A red light area is indeed a vicious circle', explains Bhaskar Banerjee, a field administrator under the SHIP project. 'Here no one can live without negotiating with those elements. And none of the elements will allow anything that will harm their interests.' In Sonagachi, pimps were not isolated individuals. They were a well-knit panchayat like a network, led by mukhiyas or headmen. The project team met with the mukhiya to present a 'win – win' argument and negotiated the support of the pimps. It became clear that the mukhiyas did not want to support the project because the pimps feared that recognising that the HIV virus was present in Sonagachi would destroy their business. But when the project team composed of sex workers (who had an equal stake in ensuring that this business was not destroyed) explained that what would destroy the business was in fact turning a blind eye to the spread of AIDS, the pimps took it seriously and more or less agreed not to resist the campaign. Similar approaches were adopted with the police and the malkins.

The police

Training for police personnel was organised after a strong partnership was established by the project with the Calcutta Police Department. The role of the All India Institute of Health and Hygiene in building this bridge was phenomenal. Till the end of April 1986, about 180 police officers had attended these training programmes. This kind of orientation enabled the police personnel to understand the 'risks' to their own lives and the lives of their families as a result of their sexual brutalities on the women of Sonagachi. This orientation, combined with the collective empowerment of the sex workers and the clients in the area, changed the state of affairs. 'The police has to think twice before hitting us', 'Aaj Thana Jane se Kursi Milte Hai, Pehle hamara case bhi register nahin hota tha', i.e. 'Today we go to the police station and we are offered a chair to sit, earlier they did not even register a case if we went to report abuse'. This qualitative indicator of success and empowerment, expressed by Putul Singh, the Secretary of the DMSC, brings out the extent of successful negotiations that have taken place between the sex workers and the structures in such a meaningful way.

The brothel owners

How do they measure their success in negotiating with the malkins? 'Well a number of malkins today keep condoms and along with the permanent clients or "babus" provide these to the customers as they come.' Other indicators include the provision of a few days off for the 'chokri', or young sex worker, especially when she is menstruating. This was not the case a few years ago. Bela didi, one of the malkins, informed us how she had opened an account in the Usha Co-operative Society for her chokris – a big stride of progress from the days, not too long ago, when Bela didi herself used to be paid nothing by her malkin. Bela didi had in fact lived in a bonded state of existence for 9 or 10 years where every penny earned was shown as used for repayment of the debt that she had incurred. What exactly was this debt? The price paid to the pimp to buy her (approximately $150), the money used to provide her clothes and cosmetics for her profession, the rent for occupying an area 10 ft by 10 ft in the brothel, and in addition, of course, food, water, electricity and medicines for STDs, etc.

From the periphery to the centre

The pattern of women's empowerment processes has been such that it has addressed almost every single development issue, be it trade, economy, environment or human rights governance. But what it has continually shied away from is addressing issues of sex and sexuality. In the last two decades HIV/AIDS has forced many groups to venture into the area of sex and sexuality, but the discomfort that most of them experience has kept the discussion at very preliminary levels, little able to contribute towards the transformation of vision, perception and attitudes related to morality and societal values. The SHIP project in Sonagachi has tried to emphasise that the struggle of the sex workers is not very different from the struggle of poor women in the informal sector. The struggle is essentially against patriarchy and domination. There are certain nuances in these struggles which are different, but the overall spirit and thrust remain the same. Both the struggles have questioned power relations, both have explored and identified vulnerabilities, both have tried to break down structures that are oppressive. The sex workers of Sonagachi have today re-examined their situation vis à vis mainstream society and have come up with some very powerful observations and insights. Mala Sinha refers to the women of mainstream society as well as the sex workers of her community as 'Dogs – it's just that one is a dog with a collar and one is without it'. Sadhna reflects on the similar levels of violence in the lives of women in mainstream society and women in Sonagachi. According to her, most relationships for women are abusive, the only difference is that sex workers can openly fight and throw the partner out, whereas a married woman suffers in silence. And as they explore edges over women in mainstream society, Minoti Dutt remarks, 'We are more liberated and free in many ways. Those husbands as passports to our identity are irrelevant.'

Over the last 7 years, the project has regularly celebrated International Women's Day, World Environment Day, World AIDS Day, participated in book fairs, flood relief programmes, sent delegations to Nepal and

Bangladesh, and to World AIDS conferences. During these exposures the sex workers have met with a range of partners from women's groups, government departments, media bodies, donors, etc. and have evolved the above-mentioned discourse on their situation within mainstream society. They have moved from the periphery to the centre, and in this process of negotiating their empowerment and safety have contributed very definitely towards maintaining wellbeing in the larger society. How have they done this? The Sonagachi movement has successfully intervened in stopping child trafficking in West Bengal. The self-regulatory boards set up this year are the mechanisms that enforce this. A number of children trafficked have been returned back to their homes and in this way the organisation is reducing vice and violence in the larger society. Thus persuasive, not confrontational, approaches have brought about real changes at multiple levels – the level of the self, the level of the peers and the level of deeply embedded structures. Their hand of friendship and support is now stretching further and further – 'even the housewives need to build their own organisation and join hands with us, otherwise they are not safe'.

Dreaming Utopia

The sex workers of Sonagachi had dreamed a dream 7 years ago. A dream to have a community sans violence, sans HIV, sans STDs, sans oppression. They had dreamt this dream at a time when it seemed utopian to most development workers. This was because the dream did not fit into the larger development context of the country and the region.

India in 1992 was entering its second medium term plan for AIDS control. The epidemiological analysis done by WHO at that point in time projected a bleak picture for the epidemic in the country. In 1994, at the World AIDS Conference in Yokohama, India was being projected as the AIDS capital of the world. With overall prevalence rates still as low as 0.8 per cent, the country was emerging with a sexual networking pattern that was quite alarming. The migration of labour both within and without, the high proportion of a sexually active population, the widening socio-economic disparities, the vulnerability of a part of its borders to the drug trade, all pointed towards an explosive epidemic in the country. The high-risk behaviour studies commissioned by the national AIDS Control Organisation in 65 cities of the country in 1994–95 only validated and confirmed the above trends.

The existence of the above factors did make the dream of the women of Sonagachi rather unreal. But by 1996, research data in this oldest and largest red light district of Calcutta showed indicators that were different. The knowledge of STDs in Sonagachi improved from 69 per cent in 1992 to 97.4 per cent in 1996; the knowledge of HIV/AIDS rose from 30.7 per cent in 1992 to 96.2 per cent in 1996. Condom usage shot up from 2.7 per cent in 1992 to 81.7 per cent in 1996. The percentage of sex workers with genital ulcers decreased from 6.2 per cent in 1992 to 2.9 per cent in 1996 and the percentage of VDRL positivity fell from 25.4 per cent in 1992 to 14.3 per cent in 1996. Above all, HIV/AIDS prevalence levels plateaued at 5 per cent when other red light areas in the country were recording a rate of 55 per cent. In fact, on 18 September 1995, the *Telegraph*, a leading daily of the country, hailed Sonagachi as the biggest brothel in Asia, with a record negative growth rate of HIV/AIDS.

The dream in fact was not quite unreal. As we talked to the women of Sonagachi, it became clear that their dream was only partly fulfilled. They were still dreaming of a world where sex work would be recognised as labour, where a majority of them over time would have entered stable marital relationships again, where the world would have redefined sex and sexuality from a feminist perspective.

Sonagachi for me came to symbolise the very best in the human spirit's search for survival, for recognition, for respect. I left Sonagachi with a number of visions in my mind – an oasis in a desert, a flame continuing to flicker in a storm, a mountaineer scaling heights and worthy women carving a niche for themselves, declaring themselves as women of worth.

Chapter Five

'I Know I am a Woman of Worth'

I am reminded of Robert Benigni's portrayal in his Oscar winning film *Life is Beautiful*. Tough, disturbing circumstances in a concentration camp and yet life could be beautiful. That, of course, was on celluloid. The focus moves to Mexico – real life, real women and a real life threat – a virus called AIDS. The report of the community-based research entitled, 'Mexican Women and the HIV/AIDS Epidemic; the intersection of Gender, Power and HIV/AIDS in Mexico', has significantly delved into what the researchers have called 'lives of challenge and achievement'.

Life with HIV/AIDS can be beautiful. This is what work in Mexico is beginning to highlight. The results of a participatory community-based research in this Central American country have been quite revealing. Forty-six women living with HIV/AIDS were interviewed separately and in groups. With ages ranging from 22 years to 54 years, this group of positive women with positive approaches represented a range of experiences, a spectrum of perceptions and motley of feelings. Nineteen were married or living with a partner, 12 were widowed and 15 women were single or separated. All had at least 6 years of formal education, with 7 having reached university level. Most of the women interviewed described a process of growing self-value and self care in spite of their commitment to taking care of their male partners and their children.

I value my life more and I try not to expose myself to getting sick. I see my life with more caring eyes. I think life is beautiful. I take care and value myself more as a woman because I know I am going to live longer and I am well . . . I love myself more.

I know I am a woman of worth. I exercise more and try not to become depressed. I take care of my health and my son's health. He is not infected.

I know that there are no victims or guilty parties. This happened to me and I have to know how to live with dignity and quality of life. I am more careful about what I eat, I don't drink, I smoke less. When I am not depressed, that is.

I take care of myself first. Before I thought of my family first, but now I understand that if I am well, they will be too. I value myself much more. I think, now that I know I have HIV, all of us need to value our body and our feelings.

These voices seem to indicate that women are coping exceptionally well with an otherwise rather debilitating disease – debilitating socially, economically, physically and emotionally.

Changes in her emotional life

What filled me with amazement as I read and re-read these quotations was that this level of self-esteem was not common in the general population in Mexico. And I say this from empirical, not anecdotal, knowledge. A comparative survey with 211 respondents in five provinces of the country covering rural and urban population used a self-esteem index to measure this aspect. Only 27.7 per cent of the women and 45.4 per cent of the men had a high self-esteem. More women (68.6 per cent) than men (43.1 per cent) had low self-esteem.

An index to measure depression was also used, based on an instrument that had been validated and used extensively in Mexico. Over twice as many women as men were severely depressed (28.6 per cent of women and 13.3 per cent of men). Women also had a higher proportion of moderate depression (54.5 per cent) as compared to men (38.8 per cent). In general, the conclusion reached was that a general lack of self-esteem and a depressed emotional state made negotiation of safer sexual practices much more difficult for women. This no doubt increased their vulnerability to HIV/AIDS in Mexico.

However, as we worked with a sample of women who were all infected with HIV/AIDS, the percentages of the depressed and the dejected seemed to be much lower in this sample of women who for all practical purposes were facing a much tougher set of circumstances. The women living with HIV/AIDS in Mexico, unlike the women living with the virus in some other countries, were depicting a higher level of self-esteem and confidence. As brought out in the table below, 36 out of the 46 women interviewed said that they took greater care of themselves and 14 out of the 46 women said that they valued themselves much more. Only 5 out of the 46 said that they did not take care of themselves and three out of the 46 said that they felt depressed due to rejection.

Table 1

Change	Number
Takes care of herself more	36
Values herself more	14
Values life more	5
Is careful to prevent infection of others	5
Takes care of herself less	5
Becomes depressed due to rejection	3
Has difficulty finding a partner	3
Has lost independence or become isolated	2

The question, therefore, that kept arising was how was it that Mexican women were displaying an increased level of self-esteem once they were diagnosed as HIV-positive?

Compassion by the community

The answers surfaced as we delved into the rich body of information that this participatory research provided. Whereas rejection and prejudice towards people living with HIV/AIDS was common, Mexico could simultaneously boast of a show of compassion and solidarity by the community towards people living with HIV/AIDS. A number of respondents in this study mentioned solidarity from family neighbours and friends. One woman described the show of solidarity she received from her neighbour. 'My neighbours all talk to me, encouraging me. They ask me if I am going to the doctor. When my husband died, since I wasn't working, they gave me milk for my son. They came over to talk; they invite me to their homes and come over for lunch to my house. They ask me to watch their kids for them. At first I was afraid they would reject me. I even thought they would chase me out of the neighbourhood, but it was exactly the opposite.' The tables below bring out the levels of rejection and social inclusion in the Mexican community towards people living with HIV/AIDS. Out of a sample of 46, 18 women had to face rejection by the community. However, what is heartening to note is that an almost equal number of people living with HIV/AIDS – about 15 in number – had also experienced a fair amount of social inclusion and solidarity in the face of the debilitating disease. This finding was different from the findings in some other countries where compassion by the community is an exception rather than a rule.

Table 2. Rejection encountered by people living with HIV/AIDS*

Offensive comments	5
None, because they don't know her diagnosis	4
Stigma related to homosexuality	3
From her partner's family (towards her)	2
From her family, towards her partner	1
Rejection by nurses	1
No one donated blood when her husband needed it	1
Someone was forced to move out of the community	1

* These included reactions the women themselves encountered, or which they observed in relation to others

Table 3. Solidarity shown towards people living with HIV/AIDS in the woman's community

From the seropositive woman's own family	4
Support from NGOs	3
Support from neighbours	2
General support and solidarity from the community	2
Existence of a home for seropositive people without their family's support	1
Recommendations by friends of which doctors to go to	1
Support from the husbands family	1
Support from affected and infected people	1

Access to counselling services

Another kind of support which was a source of resilience to women in Mexico was the availability of and access to treatment, along with counselling services. In most countries, receiving the diagnosis is the most difficult moment for the patient because it is done without providing adequate information about the disease. Health providers have little training and skills in counselling. They are, at best, able to provide some very basic clinical information. The doctors or nurses somehow find it difficult even to hide their own prejudices relating to this epidemic. 'When I went to the hospital . . . the nurses put in the I.V. (intravenous equipment) and they said something like "I am going to take a bath right away."'

Counselling for HIV/AIDS is predicated on a number of principles and values including confidentiality, privileged communication and inter-personal relationship between the counsellor and the client. Besides, counsellors and health care providers need to be equipped with well-presented and accurate information on non-clinical issues related to HIV/AIDS, for example – how can a woman take her HIV status back to the community? Who should she tell without losing love and support? How will she be able to break an abusive relationship in order to deal with her disease in an empowered fashion?

During the data collection process, one woman described her experience: 'The diagnosis was difficult, principally because I knew that it was a fatal disease but I knew nothing about the process. But as the very sensitive doctor gave me the result he said to me, "Don't worry, not everything is lost".' People living with HIV/AIDS need to know that not everything is lost if they contract the virus.

Access to medicines

In Mexico, there is an enabling policy environment in relation to the health care of people living with HIV/AIDS. It is due to this that the governmental health services, especially the Mexican Institute of Social Security, as well as the Ministry of Health, provide the essential service of distribution of anti-retroviral medications to people living with HIV/AIDS. Over half the women interviewed during this research had access to social security services, which meant that they would have access to the anti-retroviral treatment – an access that is still a dream for large numbers of women living in Asia, Africa and in many other countries of Latin America and the Caribbean. This access has undoubtedly increased the hope and the self-esteem of women living with HIV/AIDS in Mexico. Receiving information about managing HIV/AIDS through medication and self care, and in general the hope of living quite a while after the diagnosis, is of fundamental importance. However, at this juncture, it is necessary to point out that a matter of concern expressed by the researchers was that 13 out of the 46 women interviewed were not receiving anti-retroviral treatment of any kind. This occurred when neither the woman nor her partner were formally employed and so were not covered by social security benefits. The study has pointed out the need that access to medication for people living with HIV/AIDS needs to be de-linked from their employment status as this would otherwise enshrine economic inequalities and gender biases, leaving large masses of the population disadvantaged, especially as the epidemic progresses and matures in the country.

Thus, what is critical is to provide women with access to resources which can enable them to fight stress and depression and to procure adequate treatment so that their vulnerability is reduced. In fact, access to treatment and care where available is making the HIV infection a chronic disease that can be controlled for increasing periods of time.

'I am a woman.' 'I think life is beautiful.' These sentences continue to amaze me. The picture in my mind had been quite different. Today, my mind is filled with impressions that resurface again and again as I read the report. I remember I had heard women with HIV, not so long ago, say in one country of South Asia, 'To be alone and dying, yet to care for one's own HIV-infected child is a tragedy, the dimensions of which few of us can truly comprehend', and 'some people are imprisoned for life because they are HIV-positive'. 'As positive women, we are probably dealing with multiple losses and how difficult that can be whilst at the same time we are coping with the possibility of our own shattered life spans.' Women in Mexico were coping much better with the epidemic.

No doubt, this conclusion that I was drawing was based on empirical averages and did hide a lot of disparities. Nevertheless, as I looked at the sample of the study, the reasons for this 'more positive positivity' were clearer. Women who participated in the study came from all income levels. The sample was taken with the intention of overcoming any biases relating to economic disparities. The sample included women from the formal sector, from the informal sector, with low incomes as well as high incomes. Over half the women had paid employment, about one-third had additional jobs (other than their primary employment) which were usually informal and part time. About one-quarter of the sample had to quit working due to some cause related to their HIV status, either because they became sick frequently or because they migrated from a rural area to a state capital to obtain better medical services. Three women lost their jobs because of discrimination but did receive a pension and medical treatment through the social security health care system.

Access to employment

Simultaneously, analysis of the sample and the results of the study also revealed that in Mexico women living with HIV/AIDS could lead lives of dignity, positivity and enrichment, even in the most disturbing and life threatening circumstances, because a number of them were gainfully employed. About 60 per cent of the respondents had paid employment and another 25–30 per cent had work in the informal sector.

It seems from the above that the key to enable women to ride the waves of the epidemic is for policy-makers and planners to ensure that women continue to be visible in the labour market. Women's economic empowerment, manifested through their work participation rate, will need to somehow be increased to enable more women to join in the crescendo – 'I am a woman of worth'.

Table 4

Situation	Number
Women with employment	27
Women with an additional job	17
Women who stopped working due to living with HIV/AIDS	12
Women who lost their jobs due to discrimination	3
Women who began to work due to reasons related to living with HIV/AIDS	6
Someone else in the family began working related to living with HIV/AIDS	3*
Someone else in the family began working related to living with HIV/AIDS	1**
Women with young children who also had access to day care (through their own employer or spouse)	Yes/ No

*Two male partners stopped working because of their own health problems, while one lost his job because of discrimination.

** The daughter of a woman who was interviewed, who was 16 years old, left school after finishing junior high school and began working to help support the family.

The task is not easy, for the macroeconomic environment that we are facing today is producing a growth of joblessness in the wake of structural adjustment policies. People living with HIV/AIDS will continue to need jobs and so policy-makers and planners will need to look again at the criteria for selection that they had hitherto outlined for income generating programmes. These will now need to somehow include the needs of people living with HIV/AIDS and one way could be to include household dependency ratios as a key element in the selection of participants for income-generating and economic empowerment programmes. In fact, learning from the experiences of our partners and neighbours and building on the lessons already generated, it becomes imperative to remind ourselves of a warning from a well-known development worker who is now a political figure from Thailand, Mr Jon Unphakorn who as early as 1993 remarked, 'The main roots of the HIV/AIDS situation in Thailand lie in the extremely successful national development policies of the last three decades, which have focused on a rapid economic growth at the expense of all other considerations. This has brought about a widespread increase in economic and social disparities, a group of jobless citizens, a rapid depletion of natural resources and the wholesale disintegration and degradation of the rural society with its traditional qualities of economic and environmental self survivability, family and community cohesion and an in-built social welfare system.'

The ways in which we respond to the epidemic now will influence the ways in which women will participate and contribute to development in this twenty-first century. But national development will be conditional on human survival and on the survival of those who reproduce and nurture the human race. This, in fact, needs to be the primary focus of our attention today. The work in Mexico has shown us that women with HIV believe that life has to be lived and lived well, that it requires a will of steel and a resilience that makes a woman. Even when they are no more, the world will say, 'She died with dignity after teaching us what humanity is all about!'.

Chapter Six

'She Died with Dignity after Teaching us what Humanity is All About'

'She died after passing her HIV to her husband.' This is an often-repeated sentence in Zimbabwe. The echoes can be heard in homes in workplaces and in graveyards, at times shrill, at times in a hushed whisper. The tone, though, is always accusatory.

The corollary to this statement, i.e. 'He died after passing HIV to his wife', is seldom heard, perhaps only in low whispers in support groups of women living with HIV/AIDS. I assumed the reason for this state of affairs lay in the fact that since time immemorial women have been blamed for the spread of STDs. The literature of the early 1990s pointed towards this analysis. Among certain groups in Thailand and Uganda, STDs were known as women's diseases. In Swahili, the word for STDs literally means 'disease of women'. Essays on HIV/AIDS written by Ugandan school children showed how deep the prejudice was rooted. In their writings, as early as 1992–93, 40 youngsters expressed the opinion that women were mainly responsible for spreading HIV, while only three named men. These views were held by girls as well as boys, highlighting the tendency of the 'victims' of prejudice to accept its assumption as natural.

In particular, female sex workers had almost universally been characterised as 'vectors' of the disease, a description that completely ignored the role played by the customer. In the USA, in the early stages of the epidemic, many men diagnosed with HIV blamed their infection on a female sex worker. Only when interviewed at length did they admit to injecting drugs or having sex with men. The harsh judgement extended even to women who were sick and dying. 'If you have AIDS, the society rejects you. When you die you will not even be missed because you have died of a shameful disease', a married woman in Zaire told researchers. 'They will not see that maybe she remained faithful while her husband has strayed.' Given the status of women in most societies, AIDS is doubly stigmatising for most women.

Women in the forefront

As I read the report on the community-based research undertaken by a team of researchers in Zimbabwe the sentence 'She died after passing her HIV to her husband' stood out as a disturbing paradox. Why is the death of a woman being echoed so much in a society where more men are dying because of HIV/AIDS? The study carried out amongst 412 respondents recorded that 109 had lost their spouses. Of these 101 (92.7 per cent) were women compared to 8 (7.3 per cent) who were men. And just five pages further into the report I found an answer to my query. Though more men were dying of the epidemic in Zimbabwe, it was the women who were at the forefront. The caregivers interviewed during the research noted that to enable a change of attitude of the community, a number of people living with HIV/AIDS were disclosing their status – a majority of these were women. Women accepted their HIV status and tried to ensure that the community knew. Men, however, preferred to die in silence. This courageous approach manifested itself in the composition of the support groups of people living with HIV/AIDS, where there were more women as compared to men. Women were in the forefront everywhere. A large majority of the participants in income-generating projects for families affected by HIV/AIDS were also women.

Caring in the face of adversity

The profile of community caregivers also gave the epidemic a female face. As hospital infrastructure was proving to be inadequate and family institutions, both nuclear and extended, were burning out with the burden of disease and sickness, groups of caregivers from the community were springing up to respond to the needs of the hour. These caregiver groups were composed of the women of the community, young girls taken out of school to look after patients and some young boys too! With little or no resources available from the city council for the execution of their duties, these groups were improvising and responding on a day-to-day basis. In the absence of gloves and face masks, they were making do with empty plastic sugar packets. With no linen or soap available from the local government, they were straining their own household budgets to cope with the demands of the disease. From morning till evening they were bathing, feeding, cheering the sick, doing their laundry, talking about death to the children, helping in writing wills, and all this with no monetary remuneration whatsoever!

Wilson, living in the Insiza district of Zimbabwe, had been a charmer, a flirt. But then AIDS dulled his sparkle and confined him to his bed. That was when Sibongile Ndlovu increased her visits to his home, coming every day with food and caring for his bed sores. 'The whole skin on his side was coming off', she says 'and it filled his hut with a smell of sickness'. She persuaded the clinic to give her medicine and she rubbed the ointment on his raw bedsores every day for two months until he died. Four years have passed, but despite that ordeal Ndlovu is still caring for patients. How many has she assisted? 'Forty-two', she says, checking a tattered ledger with hand-written notes. How many have died? 'Sixteen.'

With little training in home-based care, these caregivers were in fact working in 'high-risk environments', with little to protect themselves against infection. And yet when asked what they would prefer, given a choice – to continue caring for the person living with HIV/AIDS in the homes or to put them in institutions – the caregivers immediately responded that they preferred to take care of the patient in his/her home. This, they said, was because the HIV/AIDS patients were not receiving enough care in the hospitals.

Dr. Lulu Muhe, heading a paediatric section of a hospital in Africa, provided a stark description of the conditions in the hospitals. Working in a ward full of children living with HIV/AIDS, Dr. Muhe had his hands in the air. 'Shortage of gloves and disposable syringes? We don't even have enough new razor blades to shave the heads of children before setting up a drip. I don't think people have any conception of the conditions we are working under. We have to perform lumbar punctures and blood trans-fusions without gloves. And to top the shortages there is the workload, which is ever increasing. We get tired and then we get careless.' The lab-oratories lack the necessary equipment, reagents and skills to make effective diagnoses. Without proper diagnosis treatment becomes difficult and sick-ness is prolonged. For instance, 'we often don't know exactly what is caus-ing the patient's diarrhoea'. The implications of this state of affairs for the women caregivers are enormous. In personal interviews, women have informed us that if the HIV/AIDS patient has diarrhoea, which is a com-mon symptom, they need 23 buckets of water per day to keep him/her clean. Time-use studies have shown that on average a woman requires 45 minutes to fetch two buckets of water in the rural areas of Asia and Africa. Despite all these conditions, committed caregivers, in institutions or out of them, were doing all they could to relieve suffering and safeguard human dignity.

And as I read the report, my eyes blurred. I stood up in salutation and began to wonder once again – what is it that makes a woman? Courage and steadfastness, compassion and love, innovation, perseverance – the list could go on.

Will traditional structures revive?

It was interesting to note from the report that there are a number of traditional support structures that are now being revived to help communities cope with the epidemic. The 'Zun de Ramambo/Isiphala Senkosi' was cited as one of the practices which had died out but was being revived in some areas. According to this practice, the chief of a village or a tribe donated a piece of land for communal use. Villagers took turns to work on that piece of land. The produce was distributed to the destitute and the needy of the village. This practice, which had died with colonisation and the introduction of social welfare, was now being revived in some provinces of Zimbabwe such as Chirumangu and Tshelanyemba. The threads of revival of such a valuable practice are, however, still quite weak. A prerequisite to the successful implementation of this practice is a healthy work force, able to produce for the sick, the elderly and the orphaned. But the work force is in fact being depleted. As an indicative window on the situation in Zimbabwe, the respondents offered a dismal picture. 'More husbands run away from their homes in order to avoid the burden of care giving to the family. Male spouses are known to come back when the partner is showing signs of recovery. On the other hand, if he falls sick when he is away, he comes back for care to his wife and remains there until he dies.'

This situation was creating a 'negative income shock', as the researchers put it, in the Zimbabwean community. Negative income shock indicated such low levels of income reached by a household in a short span of time that they were left in a state of shock and helplessness. Of the 268 respondents who were experiencing this shock, 208 (77.6 per cent) were women. The major causes of the income shock were cited as HIV-related illness by 28 per cent of the respondents, death in the family by 23 per cent and inflation by 20 per cent or the respondents. Other causes of this income shock, quoted by a small percentage of the study participants, included unemployment and income loss through care giving. If this was happening at the level of the household, the challenge that was arising was how could this be reduced or alleviated by the introduction of suitable measures at the macroeconomic level. In Zimbabwe the picture at the macro level was also very bleak and dismal. The plight of the households was in fact a reflection of the situation at the macro level.

Zimbabwe is one of the southern African countries that is severely affected by the HIV/AIDS epidemic, with a national adult prevalence rate of 25 per cent. The epidemic has already reversed hard won national health gains and continues to threaten the key development indicators of per capita income, life expectancy and literacy. Zimbabwe's economy today records a low economic growth rate of 2 per cent, a high double-digit inflation of 50 per cent and low capital access with interest rates as high as 45 per cent. A high unemployment rate of 40 per cent is therefore a natural consequence. With 250 people dying every day due to HIV/AIDS, life expectancy is hitting a low. Without HIV/AIDS, the average life expectancy in Africa in the year 2000 would have been 62 years. Instead it has fallen to 47 years. The combination of a deteriorating economic base and the onslaught of the AIDS epidemic has promoted a sharp increase in chronic poverty, that is increasingly becoming feminised.

Zimbabwe offers useful insights for countries on the threshold of the AIDS epidemic. Every indicator of development in this sub-Saharan nation is entangled with the mutating virus. The grip of the virus is pulling it back, away from progress, away from development, away from prosperity. By the year 2010 life expectancy in Zimbabwe will be less by 25 years. The child mortality rate will have been pushed up by 150 per cent. And in spite of these pulls and entanglements, the country has made progress in reducing poverty and in achieving a Human Poverty Index (HPI) value of 25 per cent. The HPI provides an aggregate human measure of the prevalence of poverty in a community. The HPI draws attention to deprivation in three essential elements of human life, namely longevity, knowledge and a decent standard of living. The HPI also reveals deprivation that would be masked if poverty was measured only by income. The scales and indices of the UNDP Human Development Report of 1999 clearly show how, amidst such dire threats to development, the Zimbabweans are moving up in the human poverty index. This indicates that in spite of very little capital availability by way of incomes, and 50 per cent of the population being income poor, in viewing poverty from a broader perspective of longevity, knowledge and a decent standard of living only 25 per cent of the Zimbabweans are poor.

In the light of the epidemic these rather redeeming statistics, brought out in the Human Development Report, have been made possible by the work of the caregivers, the women of Zimbabwe, who move like the angels of care, the apparitions of strength who are in fact the shock absorbers. In Zimbabwe, therefore, the sentence 'She died after passing her HIV to her husband', will no longer be meaningful. Folklore will have it that 'she died with dignity after teaching us what humanity is all about'.

Chapter Seven

They Learnt about the Condom after they were Infected

The attitude of the Indian community towards AIDS is strongly reminiscent of the Roman emperor Nero who fiddled while Rome burnt to ashes. Martha and Assumptha, the two gender activists who undertook a collaborative research in Tamil Nadu on gender and HIV/AIDS, have made a strong statement in their report entitled 'Community Research on Gender and HIV/AIDS'. In an indicative, not exhaustive, study it is they who pointed out that the governmental and non-governmental interventions were not extensive enough. This seems a glaring lacunae at a time when an estimated four million Indians are suspected to be carriers of the HIV virus, a situation which the development community should be geared up to. The study also pointed out that information about the protective aspects of the condom was becoming available to women after they had been infected. These were wasted efforts at a time in development history when every step needed to be calculated and intentional. The service providers targeted only those at 'high risk' for providing information on condom use and this limited the access of the general population to this kind of crucial information.

The painful refrain

Martha and Assumptha are in fact echoing the common and painful refrain of a large number of men and women in India. A woman respondent from

Chennai, aged 28 years, put the situation in a nutshell. 'I did not know much about HIV/AIDS before testing positive. The knowledge that I had about AIDS was that AIDS is a dreadful disease of promiscuous people. You can get it even by touching a person with HIV. People with AIDS are thin, with skin diseases and die soon.' A male respondent, aged 25, expressed the same concern: 'I got to know about the use of the condom only after acquiring HIV.' Whether the research was undertaken in southern India or in the northern parts of the country, whether data were collected from the east or from the western parts of India, the concern was the same.

A 37-year-old graduate living in Kanpur had no knowledge about HIV prior to acquiring the infection, which was just some 14 months earlier, when he was 35 years old. These examples are only indicative of the larger picture. About 60 per cent of the respondents questioned in community-based research in India did not know about the causes and consequences of the epidemic until they were infected or affected. This finding holds across ages, across literacy levels, across socio-economic states and across gender. Men and women, young and old, rich and poor, educated or illiterate, are being caught unawares, as the epidemic enters its second decade in the country.

Awareness creation – can it be the ultimate goal?

The initial cases of HIV/AIDS in India were reported among the sex workers of Mumbai and Chennai and the intravenous drug users of Manipur, in the mid-1980s. Since then, the disease has spread into the general population, in both urban and rural areas. Recent statistics put out by the National AIDS Control Organisation (NACO) indicate that 90 per cent of the reported cases are occurring in the sexually active and productive age group of 18–40 years (NACO 1997–98). NACO has estimated that there are 3.5 million people living with HIV in India. Until 1991, 95 per cent of the national budget for HIV/AIDS was spent on testing services. Since then, although 'awareness creation' has seemed to be the primary goal of a number of efforts in the country, the overall awareness in various sections of the population still remains very low. This low awareness about the causes and consequences of the epidemic in India could be due to the cultural sensitivity and inhibitions that hinder an open discussion about sexuality in the country. But it could also be attributed to the limitations of the awareness-raising approaches being adopted in the country by various development agencies. Not enough attention has been given to monitoring the quality of material produced and even less to assessing the impact of the different awareness-raising materials, media interventions and other approaches. Most of the visual material has failed to make the link between what was seen as a blood-borne disease and the use of condoms. The socio-cultural context, values and customs have not been adequately explored and programme implementers have failed to draw the link between these social realities and the information, education and communication (IEC) strategies that they developed to spread awareness about the epidemic.

As a result, blatant messages promoting condom use, on billboards along the highways, or on the rear bodies of buses and other public vehicles have failed to catch the attention of the Indian adolescent. As one respondent in our research rightly remarked, 'Even after getting HIV/AIDS, my husband brings home many girls and sleeps with them. I myself have seen it, but I cannot say anything about it. Since he has tied my 'tali' or wedding thread, I cannot speak against him. Being a woman, I have to accept it when he compels me to have sex with him.' And even if the anti-AIDS messages did make an impact on the young minds of boys and girls in India, could they be sure that such information would be adequate to guard them against the mutating virus when they were living in a world where young girls have little choice in the selection of their spouses? Revathy's testimony brings out the dilemmas and vulnerabilities of young women in India trying to live precariously in the twilight zone of the old traditions and the new social order.

Revathy was from a poor family married into an upper middle class family. Unable to gather enough resources to provide for the necessary 'dowry', Revathy's mother married her off to a man whose proposal for marriage had come through a marriage broker. Revathy was neither prepared for the marriage nor liked it, but had no choice. After her marriage, Revathy had just one unprotected sexual encounter with her husband. On the third day of her marriage, her husband started falling ill and had persistent fever. A routine HIV test was done and he tested positive for HIV/AIDS. He now remains in a semi-conscious state but is looked after day and night by Revathy, who does this not out of love or affection for the man but mere consideration. Revathy is convinced that her in-laws knew about the HIV status of their son even before he was married which is why they had got him married in a hurry without asking for dowry. Revathy cried bitterly the day she learnt that she had also tested positive. She had hoped that the result of her blood test would be negative, as the only exposure she had had to the virus was the one unprotected intercourse with her husband. Revathy is in love with another man, but does not want to remove her 'tali', or wedding chain, as she fears that such an act would cause the death of her husband.

I felt a sudden sting of pain, of anger, of hopelessness as I read Revathy's testimony. It was real. I had met and seen a number of Revathys in India but her words lingered in the air around me with a heaviness that is difficult to explain or put down in words. Facts and figures about the epidemic kept appearing and reappearing in my mind. There is usually a less than one per cent chance of getting infected per unprotected intercourse provided the woman has a healthy genital tract without cuts or lesions. Cuts and lesions are normally caused by sexually transmitted infections. Such infections in India are rampant, especially amongst people living in poverty as they can be caused by the inability to use a clean cloth during menstruation and lack of cleanliness in the genital areas in conditions of water scarcity. STDs in India are the third largest cause of death after tuberculosis and malaria. And in spite of knowing that, we as development workers have failed to empower women with information and other resources that could help to guard them from the onslaught of the epidemic.

Still in the same pit

In 13 states surveyed in 1992/93, only one in six women said that they had heard of HIV/AIDS. In 1992, the level of AIDS awareness amongst women in three fairly densely populated states, where the so-called aware-ness efforts had been going on for more than half a decade, was dismal.

Table 5

	Population in millions	% who had heard of HIV/AIDS
West Bengal	68.1	10
Maharashtra	78.9	19
Tamil Nadu	55.9	23

Source: World Vision Relief and Development, Quarterly Report 1992. Article by Asha Bhende

Today, 8 years later, we are still stuck in the same mud pit. The research has revealed that in Assam 98.5 per cent of respondents have little or no knowledge about HIV. Reports from four Indian states read as follows:

'He left his job and broke all contact with his colleagues. One day he was found dead on a footpath.' Case c-10 – Assam.

'The first client that I met in the hospital informed me that he is HIV-positive and soon I found out that he was not sure what "being positive" entails. The hospital staff neglected him, nobody wanted to inject him, the injections are still lying there.' Case c-1 – Assam.

'His family members did not turn up when he was admitted to the hospital for treatment. She [his wife] alone had to take care of him. After his death, her mother-in-law asked her to leave the house and denied her any share in the property. Her mother-in-law also told her to kill her three-year-old daughter. Even now she has to hear her neighbours say, "Your husband was a bad and dirty man".' To avoid hearing this, and to stay away from unnecessary fights, she prefers staying indoors and has isolated herself. Her children do play with the other children but the neighbours fear that their house is infected.' Case 24 – Delhi.

'My aunt consulted the astrologer who informed us that someone had administered witchcraft to our family. Last time when I went to the village, I was asked to drink the juice of drumstick leaves. I vomited and they said the witchcraft was now out. I do not know whether to believe it or to doubt it.' 25-year-old woman – Andhra.

These instances can all be clubbed under one major concern – that of misinformation and disempowerment. How long will women and men continue to accept that their basic human rights can be ignored by those in positions of responsibility and at the cutting edge to make change happen? In a world where rights are seen as entitlements the blame for the number of lives and livelihoods at risk today lies squarely on the doorsteps of the change-makers, be they from the government or from the community. Armchair criticism may be an intoxicating pastime; it cannot be an antidote. We need to act and demand an adherence to ethical and human rights principles. We need to create a critical mass of empowered rights-seekers. With more and more women getting infected the women's movement will need to take this challenge by the horns – demanding information where information is due. Without this more mothers will be infected, more girls will be uneducated, more households will witness a feminisation of poverty. More women will be pushed out of families to live as single and deserted women.

This would be a rational attitude to adopt. Instead hysteria prevails. Outraged holier-than-thou moralists twist the entire argument with their chant – 'God's plan was for Adam and Eve, not for Adam and Steve!' All we hear is people arguing about homosexuals, prostitutes and higher morality. We need to talk about how to provide succour to the patient, about pre-emptive measures, about how to fight a fatal disease, about institutional health care and a long-term policy to enable people to live and die with dignity. We need to revisit our own stereotypes, we need to reconceptualise the definition of the family to include those who are marginalised like, homosexuals and single women. Above all, we need to acknowledge that HIV/AIDS is a structural problem – a problem arising out of deep-rooted cultural settings in the society. Awareness creation in keeping with the individual's right to information is merely a first step. A series of initiatives needs to be launched to break and rebuild gender-friendly and more egalitarian structures. These require new alliances, expanded partnerships and innovative approaches that can create the ripples of change.

Chapter Eight

Ripples of Change

An active involvement with the women's movement since the early 1980s had over time created a sense of arrogance and conceit within me. As gender was a cross-cutting issue, we who considered ourselves the 'gender experts' assumed we knew everything about development once we had acquired the skill of mainstreaming gender concerns in the various development sectors. A rude shock jolted me as I moved into the area of HIV/AIDS. Work on this rather 'unrecognised' sphere required a very deep understanding of sex and sexuality. It was not long before I realised how little I knew, or in fact had ever wanted to know, about this aspect of a woman's life. It seemed strange how both from within and from without there was a resistance – a feeling of bearing an illegitimate child. It required an effort and a deliberate breaking down of inhibitions. How could I be seen working with sex workers and gay men? How could I use, or even read, the rather obscene and degenerate words, be they three-lettered or four-lettered. It was quite a change from being the utopian sociologist, a part of a large movement working out details at the micro and the macro levels on how the revolution would transform the oppressed status of women, envisioning a society in which the distinctions between the 'masculine' and the 'feminine' would be eliminated. Now I was moving into working with an unknown or at best marginalised constituency of people living with stigma and shame, isolated and abused.

Any discussion with possible partners seemed so value loaded, so emotional, so culturally mediated. Searching inwards, I soon realised a secrecy, a discomfort and a denial relating to my own perceptions about my sexuality. Was I in a position to exercise good judgement in this field of HIV/AIDS? Was sexuality intertwined in my mind with morality? Was I in agreement with and was I promoting the concepts outlined by the gender-based construction of sexuality?

As I explored and as I meditated on these issues I realised that I needed to unlearn and then relearn the concepts of sex and sexuality before I could work with people living with HIV/AIDS in a manner that was meaningful and accountable. Conceit and complacence crumpled under the strain of ignorance and the rebuilding began, slowly, brick by brick, layer by layer. My education began with visits to red light areas, in India and in the Philippines, which opened my eyes to a vista of issues regarding women. These issues seemed so alien; I had not even considered them in my entire career in development work. Lessons were imparted to me over luncheon discussions with gay men in ghettos or in global conferences. Gliding through gay bars in Sydney threw up posers which I had not addressed before. I spent hours observing de-addiction processes in the drug rehabilitation centres in Myanmar, worked with people living with HIV/AIDS on quilt projects in Hong Kong and moved in the slums of Nairobi amongst shackled and dilapidated houses housing women living with HIV/AIDS. I visited women infected with the virus in the villages of Nepal. I held discussions with researchers. All this became a part of the process of rebuilding and reconstruction. Once this had been done, a search for partners began.

By the mid-1990s, the lessons learnt from the epidemic in Africa had shown that NGOs were perhaps the critical change agents in this area of HIV/AIDS. Outpatient advice and home care was the model that seemed to be delivering the greatest benefits for people affected by the epidemic. Communities needed to be mobilised and supported and in this the role of civil society organisations was of prime importance. The reality, however, was quite different. My search for partners revealed that less than one per cent of the NGOs working on development were working on HIV/AIDS. The situation was the same in practically every country in Asia. In India in 1994, we could identify 728 NGOs working on the issue, out of over 100,000 registered NGOs. In Nepal, the figure stood at 90 of the 6000 registered civil society bodies. In the Philippines, only around 2 per cent of development NGOs were including HIV/AIDS concerns in their work. Country after country revealed a similar picture. What, then, was the future of the issue without the active participation of civil society? The future looked dismal; we needed to probe the causes of this bleak reality.

A questionnaire sent out to a number of NGOs enquiring about the reasons for this lack of interest in HIV/AIDS resulted in some interesting revelations. 'We do not want to work on the issue of HIV/AIDS because it affects very few individuals', said some NGO partners. Others remarked 'It is a health issue and NGOs dealing with health can deal with it. Why should all of us be working on it?' Yet others proclaimed 'If we work on this issue, the police will be after us – after all how can we be seen working with gay men and sex workers?' Another revelation emerged as the NGOs explained, 'We do not have the skills to work on the epidemic'. The issues raised were not only revealing, they were essentially intriguing. What were the kinds of skills required? I enquired through a series of focus group discussions in 8 countries of Asia and came to the conclusion that skills on how to talk about sex and sexuality, how to help HIV-affected households to take sound financial decisions when disease sets in and how to manage an HIV-positive person with local resources at home were some of the key issues.

The issues to be dealt with were becoming clear, as though the mist was lifting. There was misinformation in civil society regarding the HIV/AIDS virus. More than a decade into the epidemic it was still being perceived as a health issue. The epidemiology of the virus remained an

enigma to large numbers of development workers. The numbers of identified AIDS victims still continued to deceive human understanding about
the magnitude of the problem. There was a need to shift the focus of
understanding of the epidemic from the 'individual' to the 'community',
as risk-associated behaviours such as unprotected sexual intercourse or
sharing equipment among injecting drug users were largely seen as individually not socially driven.

With these challenges, a pilot initiative in India, entitled
'Strengthening Community Based Responses to HIV/AIDS in India', was
launched. The history of this project dates back to 1995, when a situa-
tional and needs assessment of NGOs in India in relation to the epidemic
was conducted. The report drew attention to the need for increasing partnership between government and NGOs and also to the need for capacity
building among NGOs. This was critical to expand the response to the
epidemic. The situation and needs assessment also clearly revealed that
80 per cent of the funds channelled through NGOs had been used for
awareness-building and condom promotion programmes for over half a
decade and yet there was little evidence of any kind of behavioural
change among the communities. It was clear that the approaches adopted
had relied on the assumption that the fundamental problem to be
addressed was one of lack of knowledge and that the provision of information in itself would lead to a change of behaviour.

Hence, drawing upon the experience of other health and development issues such as population and reproductive health, countries had
invested in large-scale 'IEC' campaigns, sometimes in combination with
more focused educational campaigns for specific susceptible groups. The
large-scale nature of these activities resulted in content which tended to
be general, rather than specific, simple, rather than complex, and exter-
nally determined, rather than locally generated. Not surprisingly, the
impact evaluation of these efforts consistently revealed significant potential in terms of creating changes in awareness but much less convincing

evidence to demonstrate impact on behaviour.

Another broad conclusion was that the risk of HIV associated with behaviour was 'social' in nature, involving more than one person and occurring within specific social, cultural and economic settings. An enhanced understanding of the socio-economic causes and consequences of the epidemic among the community was necessary to reduce risk behaviour within both social and economic contextual realities.

By 1996, many NGOs in India, frustrated over the lack of effectiveness of IEC and awareness-raising campaigns, were willing to explore alternative educational approaches based on participatory principles which could sustain the learning process and render it more useful in creating capacities to prevent the spread of HIV/AIDS in the country. As Prakriti, an NGO in India, put it: 'To make people accept their vulnerability, acceptance has to come from within themselves. Time and time again, an empathetic non-judgmental democratic approach has worked where no amount of top down teaching has succeeded.'

In an environment that was receptive, the charming and convincing Lyra Srinivasan partnered us in our efforts and visited a number of NGOs. During 1996–97 attention was drawn to the potential of participatory approaches in influencing human behaviour by enhancing understanding about HIV/AIDS in India. In her subtle, unassuming yet persuasive style, Lyra developed and demonstrated to a group of NGOs a number of participatory learning tools of relevance to the epidemic. Above all, she explained the principles of participatory learning.

The first and the foremost tenet was respect for the individual as an adult with experience, ideas and concerns of his/her own. In line with this principle, substantive content is not imposed on adults but opportunities are provided for them first to tap their own rich experience and then to identify issues and situations requiring further analysis. They are thus participants in a process in which, in lieu of an instructor, there is a facilitator who encourages group participation, and learns much more from the group's sharing of experience. To ensure that this happens, the facilitator avoids beginning the session with a lecture, but instead engages the participants with a task which they can all freely engage in. This may include defining their own ground rules on attendance and participation in the sessions.

The second tenet was ensuring an enabling environment in which the participants felt comfortable in expressing their ideas and in supporting or challenging each other if they so wished. This is particularly important in a sector such as HIV where sensitive issues are likely to come up concerning sex and sexuality, stigma, gender power relations, blame and hostility, personal income losses, family crisis and pain. To create and maintain this type of enabling environment, in which all the participants can feel safe in being open and honest, the facilitator makes sure that all vestiges of hierarchical relationships are removed. This applies even to the room arrangement and to the positioning of tables and chairs, thus allowing the participants to move around and constitute sub-groups of different sizes more easily than if they were all facing a head table as the focus of control.

The third tenet was the use of non-conventional discussion media, i.e. pictures, cut-out figures, 'chits', props or other aids which the participants themselves can manipulate, sort out, prioritise, modify and interpret as they wish. This is another means of equalising communication opportunities and helping to uncover talents within the group which might otherwise not be disclosed in a more formal stratified set-up. The tools give all members of the group a chance to be involved in some way since, for example, it takes many different talents to create a mural, take part in role playing, or actively engage in group problem-solving. The aids also help to liven up the session, providing scope for creativity, analysis, planning and sometimes even humour.

The informal consultation led to the organisation of a training workshop for NGO representatives on HIV and development. The informal consultation enriched a group of NGOs working on HIV/AIDS issues in India with concepts relating to participatory approaches and the HIV and development workshop provided information on the socio-economic causes and consequences of the epidemic to a large group of NGOs in the country who have been working on participatory approaches for over a decade but not essentially on the epidemic. This suddenly expanded the pool of partners in India who could work effectively on the epidemic with an in-depth understanding about HIV/AIDS using participatory methods and approaches.

I could actually feel the expanding ripples as I prepared for the HIV and development workshop for our NGO partners in India. The process had begun; the smaller ripples were now producing larger ripples. The interest in the issue was overwhelming. I sat there in the conference room struck with amazement and wonder. These were the very NGOs who had categorically informed me not too long ago that HIV/AIDS was not that important a development concern and asked 'Why should all of us be working on it?' And yet the use of participatory methodologies as learning tools had generated a unique interest and commitment in the same group of our partners. With barely a skeletal support from donor agencies, amounting to just $400, driven by motivation, the NGOs took over the process to expand the ripples. Similar workshops were organised in 7 states of the country, not by facilitators recruited by the donors, but by the NGOs themselves. These events soon galvanised the creation of a planning group for the initiative within the country. This planning group was composed of 8–10 umbrella NGOs who became the driving force for the effort as more and more trainers were oriented in the use of participatory learning tools.

The tools were exciting and innovative but, above all, were prepared and owned by the planning team. The tool entitled 'Sex and Sexuality' imparted the much-needed skill of how to talk about sex and sexuality. Coupled in pairs, the participants discussed the most intimate part of their lives as they responded to the following key questions:

❖ Recall the first time you heard the word 'sex'. How old were you and how did you feel about discussing the subject?

❖ Recall the first time you asked someone about sex and under what circumstances?

❖ Have you ever seen yourself naked in front of a mirror? What were your feelings about your body?

And as they completed their conversation with the facilitator, freely expressing their views, further reflection was provoked by issues like 'what sexual information do you still lack today?'

The learning tools used were amazing

Whether it was the 'Fleet of Hope' or the 'Story of Maya' or the 'unserialised posters', the training sessions stimulated very active light-hearted and non-confrontational discussions. The 'Women's Balloon Exercise' promoted group reflection on the many interrelated factors which determine the impact of HIV/AIDS.

Discussions were held on women's wellbeing and productivity, and on ways of empowering them to play an optional role in the epidemic's collective prevention and support effort. Perhaps the tools that evoked maximum interest and fascination were the 'Demographic Silhouettes'. Through multiple sets of cardboard cut-outs, silhouette figures of men, women and children representing 9 different age groups, an awareness was generated about the gender-focused causes and consequences of HIV/AIDS. In the spirit of participation and acknowledgement of the pool of learning available in the country, Lyra had remarked, 'these tools are not perfect and were never intended to be. They can only be sharpened and perfected through experience. Each try out brings new insights and points to more exciting possibilities. Questions will always provoke healthy inquiry, why use three discussion groups instead of two or even one? Do discussions in a lighter vein tend to belittle the seriousness of the issues arising from the epidemic? Questions of this kind and more await experimentation and feedback by trainers everywhere. The only requirement is that they take the time to document and share the insights they acquire in the process.'

Lyra's words ring true. Today, in 6 states of India, NGOs have framed dynamic action plans strengthening their counterparts in the government, in civil society and in other training bodies with these techniques. The initiative is no longer a capacity development effort, it has acquired the status of a movement. Larger issues relating to government–NGO partnership in preventing the spread of HIV/AIDS are being discussed and debated. Release of funds in support of the proposed action plans when it is being processed in large bureaucratic set-ups, be they national or international bodies, has taken time. But the work goes on.

Looking back at the series of events that culminated in the training of trainers and the formulation of state action plans to expand the community-based response to the epidemic, the entire process seems long, tedious and cumbersome. Perhaps this was so because we chose the consultative processes over top down approaches. Cajoling, convincing, encouraging our partners has not been easy. Moving away from IEC approaches to mobilisation for social change has taken its toll of individual capacities in spite of this tradition being particularly rich in India. But what I keep asking myself as I write is: 'Could it have been any way other than this?'

The initiative is not devoid of problems and dilemmas. Government support for this initiative has been surprisingly low. It is often said that the forces that actively work towards protecting the status quo resist any attempt to bring about systemic changes. However there are examples where strong and dynamic leaders in organisations have been able to make a beginning. It all depends on our ability to build a strong pressure group to force the leadership to acknowledge the need for change in order to achieve its own stated objectives. The processes set in motion have created ripples of change. We hope that the tools prepared and disseminated will empower the disempowered to not only analyse and express their reality but, as Robert Chambers has said, ' to put the reality first'. Unless this is done the epidemic is on track to dwarf all other catastrophes.

Chapter Nine

On Track to Dwarf every Catastrophe

Not too long ago, in early 1997, I was working closely with the United Nations Development Programme and the National AIDS Programme of Nepal. The number of AIDS cases written in white chalk on a small blackboard in the room of the Director of the National AIDS Programme was 546. I remember the light-hearted laugh of the Director as he commented, 'Ms Nath, HIV/AIDS is just one bus accident for us. It is not a catastrophe'. Perhaps countries in other parts of the world were experiencing similar manifestations of the 'denial syndrome'. A study in 1997, undertaken by UNAIDS and Harvard, showed that in that year the international donor countries devoted only $150 million to AIDS prevention in Africa. This was less than the cost of making the Hollywood extravaganza, called *The Wild West*! This was in fact the cost of building 12 kilometers of a double track motorable highway in the United States of America.

Today, in the morgue of Parirenyatwa Hospital in Zimbabwe, head mortician Paul Tabvemhini opens the door to the large cold room that holds dead bodies. But it is impossible to walk in because so many bodies lie on the floor; wrapped in blankets from their deathbeds or dressed in the clothes they died in. Along the walls, corpses are packed two to a shelf. In a second cold storage area the shelves are narrower, so Tabvemhini faces a gruesome choice. He can stack the bodies one on top of each other, which squashes the face and makes it hard for relatives to identify the body or he can leave them out in the hall unrefrigerated. He refuses to deform the bodies so a pair of corpses lies outside on gunnys behind a curtain. The odour of decomposition is faint but clear. This in fact is the level of the AIDS catastrophe in Africa.

There is no reason why the tragedy or catastrophe should be any different in the other regions – it is perhaps only a matter of time. The wide crescent of east and southern Africa that sweeps down from Mount Kenya and around the Cape of Good Hope is the hardest hit. Here the virus is cutting down more and more of Africa's most energetic and productive people aged between 15–49.

According to a recent analysis undertaken by the World Bank in Africa, AIDS will have killed 15,000 teachers in Tanzania by the year 2010 and the training of new teachers to replace them will require $37.8 million. In Côte d'Ivoire a teacher dies every school day. In Zimbabwe half of the patients in hospitals are infected by HIV/AIDS. Kenya will need to spend half of its national budget to treat HIV/AIDS. Households in Côte d'Ivoire are already experiencing a 67 per cent drop in income because of HIV/AIDS. Between 20–30 per cent of workers in South Africa's gold mining industry – the mainstay of the country's economy – are estimated to be HIV-positive; replacing these workers will cut into the industry's productivity.

Catastrophes and challenges have riddled human history over the ages. The challenge that this epidemic is posing is unique. For example, the slave trade also targeted people in their prime, killing or sending into bondage perhaps 25 million people. But that happened over four centuries. Seventeen years have passed since the AIDS virus was first found in Africa on the shores of Lake Victoria, yet the virus has already killed more than 11 million people in Africa alone. Close to 23 million people in Africa are now living with the virus.

War and conflict are no doubt catastrophic. Last year the combined wars in Africa killed 200,000 people. AIDS has killed ten times that number in the same region over the same span of time.

Other catastrophes – floods, famines, earthquakes, volcanic eruptions – kill large numbers of people in one swift sweep, leaving behind pain and agony, but in the wake of the HIV/AIDS epidemic these environmental disasters seem, to me, much easier to cope with. They have a certain level of in-built resistance for the affected. Food aid, rehabilitation opportunities like credit assistance, medical assistance, setting up of refugee establishments, above all a kind of sympathy, love, concern and affection make reconstruction possible. I have met victims of disasters caused by earthquakes, floods and famine, and they do reminisce about the tragedy of the past, but they seem to be able to look at it as a pain left behind. The tumultuous moments faced as a result of mass dislocations of populations amidst massacre and terror are related by the victims of such tragedies with an almost anecdotal value and spirit. The events are usually dramatised and told by grandparents to their grandchildren, and often used to stir a sense of gratitude in the next generation for not having gone through those moments. These tragedies often bring with them an in-built resilience. As I relate this my mind is conjuring up the vision of the Indo-Pak conflicts, the stories of the partition of the two countries related to me by my grand-uncles, who lived through it all, lost a lot but regained all that was lost in less than a generation. I do not see this kind of resistance in households and nations reeling under the shock of the HIV/AIDS epidemic. The epidemic is truly on track to dwarf every catastrophe. In other catastrophes the worst consequence is death, in HIV/AIDS the worst consequence is not just the dead, but the living who are left behind.

According to Geoff Foster, the founder of the Family AIDS Caring Trust (FACT): 'The orphans of the AIDS epidemic are more likely to be poor, more likely to be deprived of education, more likely to be abused, neglected and stigmatised and when they get HIV and die who will care for their children? Nobody, because they will be children of orphans with no grandparents.' The immensity of this catastrophe was brought out with stark data analysis by Dr. Mechai Viravaidya on the floor of the UN when he declared that there had been a 400 per cent increase in orphans in Cambodia, a 300 per cent increase in Vietnam and Myanmmar, and that in his own country, Thailand, by the end of the year 2000 there would be 90,000 orphans. I heard Mechai in astonished silence. The adage that 'it took a village to raise a child' seemed to fade away from my consciousness. The projections go on. Ms Eimi Watanabe, the Assistant Secretary General of the UNDP highlighted the catastrophe on World AIDS Day in 1999: 'Before HIV/AIDS was on the horizon one in 50 children were orphaned, but today it is one in 10 and by 2010 it has been projected that in some countries in sub-Saharan Africa one in every three children will be orphaned.' She was quoting from empirical work recently undertaken by the World Bank in the African region.

In 2000, the South African researcher, Martin Schontiech published a paper that begins by noting 'In a decade's time every fourth South African will be aged 15–24. It is in this age group that people's propensity to commit crime is at its highest. While some causes of crime can be curtailed, other causes such as large numbers of juveniles in the general population and a high proportion of children brought up without adequate parental supervision, are beyond the control of the state. No amount of state spending on the criminal justice system will be able to counter this harsh reality.'

More AIDS and more crime are among the most dramatic consequences of the orphan explosion. An increasingly poor population experiencing intergenerational poverty and less investment by the capitalists in countries with mature epidemics is crippling any possibilities for the alleviation of human suffering.

Today, every minute, 5 more people under the age of 25 are being infected. More than half of these are women living in the developing world. These women are facing a host of ethical dilemmas as they confront the HIV/AIDS epidemic. I echo a few of their concerns and anxieties. Should they risk giving birth to a sick child? Can they ever get access to protocol 076 that could prevent this from happening? Would they be cheated and used as a placebo if they volunteered to participate in research trials? Will their child die if they did not breast feed him/her for fear of mother-to-child transmission? Will their community forgive them for not breast-feeding their child? If they do opt for not bringing a sick child into this world who will ensure that they have access to a safe medical termination of pregnancy?

What gives meaning to our work is that these are only dilemmas and not dead ends. The dilemmas do have answers and these answers can be found if we decide to re-engineer development with the richness of the perspectives of people living with HIV/AIDS. For me, the story of the epidemic is none other than a story of lives shattered by tragedies and lives rekindled with hope.

Esther's Story

Working with development issues there comes a time when one gets a little frustrated. It's difficult to mark success. Sometimes we do not know for years whether the work done has made a change or touched a life. That is one reason why Esther's story has so much meaning for me. But that, of course, is not the only reason. Esther's story is perhaps the landmark milestone from tragedy towards hope.

Esther's story is real.

The year – 1998. The place – a doctor's clinic. The purpose – a check up for her sick child . . . and it was then that lightning struck. Her sick child needed a blood transfusion and she gave her sample. The sequence of events seem almost like a third-class soap opera. The doctor informed her that she and her child were both HIV-positive. Bewildered and scared, she asked him what to do. He callously replied that she could not do much as AIDS could not be cured and anyway she would not live long. Esther's nightmare was far from over. She turned to her husband for solace and support but he left her after coming to know that she was HIV-positive. Esther spent the next four years in agony, in pain, in despair. Until she came across a newspaper clipping which read 'HIV/AIDS – THERE IS HOPE'. There was a phone number and a name beneath the heading. Esther wasted no time and spoke on the number to Linda Francis, a social worker at the organisation called 'THE CENTER'.

Then life changed. She was told categorically that being HIV-positive does not mean that one was dying. After long hours of counselling Esther emerged a much stronger and a more positive human being. Today Esther is employed as a counsellor. She is not dead as had been predicted, instead she is more alive than many of us.

Esther's story is not hers alone – this is the story of many AIDS victims across the divide. They have lived through it all – pain, rejection, desolation and fear. They have triumphed over them, to move from tragedy towards hope.

Chapter Ten

Lives Shattered by Tragedy and Rekindled with Hope

A rmchair philosophising is an intoxicating pastime. We often tend to argue over past tragedies, hoping to draw lessons from events that have passed. Could the lives of more than 6 million Jews have been saved had the railway tracks that led to Auschwitz been bombed? Could the partition of a strong south Asian nation have been prevented by timely counselling of the headstrong leader? Could the Vietnam war have been shortened by the creation of strong lobbies in the civil society of the USA? Could the two million Cambodians who were slaughtered by a mad dictator have been saved by aiming to eliminate the political dictator Pol Pot and his party, the Khmer Rouge? I have often wondered why these discussions are held after the worst is over and solutions offered in hindsight. Discussions held after the event can only be intellectual debates. They cannot be an antidote. In search of an answer, I have often pondered and felt that these kinds of humanitarian tragedies bring with them a sense of responsibility and an ensuing guilt for us all.

The situation is no different in the case of HIV/AIDS. The epidemic is constantly and repeatedly asking us just one question, 'Are you human?' We try to put up all our defences, snap out of our apathy, but the query is relentless. 'Are you human?' 'What verdict will your descendants pass on you if you stand by silently while a generation of children is reduced to a biological underclass by this sexual holocaust?' In sheer tiredness and guilt we have been stirred into action. Perhaps this explains the upswell of interest after more than a decade of relative apathy towards the issue of the HIV/AIDS epidemic.

Propelled by the same compulsion, on the tenth day of the first month of the new millennium, the UN Security Council turned its powerful attention to the epidemic. It signalled an international recognition that the problem of the AIDS epidemic could no longer be ignored. The Security Council had never before dealt with a health issue. The issue of HIV/AIDS was proclaimed as an issue of human security and not just an issue of health alone. The Security Council was now signalling to the national leaders and the heads of private corporations that they must get their priorities right. Lives had been shattered by tragedies, but now these lives needed to be rekindled with hope.

I sat in the Security Council listening to the statements being made. The Executive Director of the UN Joint and Co-sponsored Programme on HIV/AIDS, Dr. Peter Piot, outlined the enormity and urgency of the problem. Ambassador Holbrooke, the Permanent Representative of the USA to the UN, stated, 'In my view the first requirement is to destigmatise the disease. All Americans will remember when Nancy Reagan held the AIDS baby; it was a major step towards destigmatisation. The epidemic threatens not only human lives but also the entire human community.' Vice President Al Gore declared that his participation in this unprecedented event was due to his long track record of arguing that national security in the post-Cold War world went much beyond its narrower definition. The Health Minister of Zimbabwe questioned the logic of the developed world in spending $600 billion on the millennium bug, a virtual virus, and only $150 million in Africa on the HIV virus, a real virus that was growing exponentially and shattering the lives and livelihoods of men, women and children. In the same august chamber, the representatives of developing countries were raising questions filled with anger and indignation, 'Why was treatment for HIV/AIDS concentrated in the countries of the north, when the patients were in the countries of the south? Was this not another form of ethnic cleansing? When and how would pharmaceutical companies take responsibility and make drugs accessible and affordable to those who needed them the most? A fund for this kind of therapeutic solidarity needed to be created, suggested France. When would a vaccine be developed, considering that the international donor community had allocated $300 million a year for this purpose? Heated debates, arguments and counter arguments were put forth on very pertinent issues.

The chamber of the Security Council in the UN building in New York is a chamber that for me had always been void of any real humanitarian feeling. Its membership, I had felt, was politically orchestrated, its discussions were politically manoeuvred and its conclusions were politically biased. But on 10 January 2000, my impressions underwent a sudden transformation. I could see a new Security Council emerging in this era of HIV/AIDS. It is axiomatic that predictions of humanitarian tragedy rarely compel the world to mass action. On 10 January this axiom was being proved wrong. The chamber of the Security Council had suddenly become alive as mere facts and figures were transformed into a call for action. Hope was once again being rekindled.

For me the event had astronomical implications. Earlier, as an activist and then as an employee of the United Nations, trying to champion the cause of people living with HIV/AIDS had always been an uphill drive. Lack of political commitment had always been the bottleneck to sincere efforts and their sustainability. This event had finally put the issue of HIV/AIDS on the world's radar screen.

My elation on this day was, however, tarnished. It was not absolute. Why? Because the entire debate remained blind to the gender dimensions of the epidemic. Except for the 'reading out' of some very basic data on prevalence disaggregated by gender, there was no attention drawn to the unquestionable need to put the concerns of women on the global agenda in a world where the epidemic was now empirically proving to affect women more negatively than men. Gender inequalities were being exacerbated by the epidemic and it was now growing and taking roots in the cracks and crevices of these inequalities. What was most disturbing was that a number of the member states present in the Security Council on this momentous day had also been associated not too long ago, in fact less than a year earlier, with a resolution on the girl child and HIV/AIDS, passed and endorsed by 45 UN member states, as a result of an active intergovernmental process, at the forty-third session of the Commission on the Status of Women, in March 1999.

In its resolution 43/2, dated March 1999, on 'Women, the Girl Child and the Human Immunodeficiency Virus/Acquired Immunodeficiency Syndrome', the Commission on the Status of Women had noted the growing proportion of women being infected with HIV in every region, especially among the younger age groups. The Commission had asked governments, relevant UN agencies, funds and programmes, intergovernmental and non-governmental organisations, individually and collectively, to make every effort to make combating HIV/AIDS a priority and to implement effective prevention strategies and programmes. It had called, in particular, on the international community to intensify its support of national efforts against HIV/AIDS, particularly in favour of women and girls. The intergovernmental body had invited the UN Secretary General to report to the Commission on the status of women in its forty-fourth session. The Commission had urged governments, with the assistance of the relevant UN agencies, funds and programmes, to adopt a long-term timely and coherent AIDS prevention policy with a public information and education programme specifically tailored to the needs of women and girls within their socio-cultural contexts, keeping in mind the sensitivities and special needs in their lives.

Why then was so little attention being paid to the gender dimensions of the epidemic at the UN Security Council? The onus of blame and responsibility falls on us, as we have perhaps underestimated the level of advocacy needed to make these issues central to any discourse.

The resolution of the forty-third session of the Commission on the Status of Women and the discussion in the Security Council on the HIV/AIDS epidemic has created a normative environment. This can enable affirmative action to refocus the monitoring of the epidemic into different groups, with attention to the implicit gender biases in current surveillance procedures. The new focus should definitely include the younger age groups with a systematic gender disaggregation. The lower average age of infection among women as compared to men makes this a priority. Similarly, a closer integration of the monitoring of the HIV/AIDS epidemic with data collection on maternal and child mortality will highlight areas where AIDS-related deaths are currently being missed. This is because there is a possibility that female deaths caused by AIDS are marked by mortality associated with other causes of maternal death, and infant mortality may go similarly undetected, leading to inaccurate assumptions about HIV among mothers. At present the detection of the epidemic is biased. Men living with HIV are detected more readily than women are. This is because whereas sero-prevalence surveys reach men in the general population through samples drawn from the military, prisoners, etc., such surveys for the detection of the number of women living with HIV are conducted only in antenatal clinics. This does not take into account fertility differences between HIV-positive and HIV-negative women. It also ignores the realities that surround sexual networking patterns within the framework of a gender-based construction of sexuality, for example the assumption that housewives are not at risk of contracting the virus.

The above-mentioned international instruments and historic events have also cleared the ground for a gender sensitive re-examination of the legal and ethical environment surrounding the lives of people living with HIV/AIDS. Today there is reason to believe that the creative use of law, based on an appreciation of complex social values, may be able to bring about changes so that the abuse of human rights is minimised, if not altogether eliminated. The law can, therefore, play an important role in seeking to change the underlying values and patterns of social inter-actions that create vulnerability to the HIV/AIDS epidemic.

At the very onset, we need to examine with a gender-sensitive lens the laws relating to the prevention and suppression of sex work; the laws that reduce women's access to productive assets, for example, the laws on inheritance, marriage, divorce and traditional sexual practices; the policies or laws regulating sex education in schools; and the rules relating to the professional and ethical orientation of service providers. The process, we are convinced, will not be an exercise in futility. What is needed is to make the discussion as broad-based as possible. It was this kind of broad-based dialogue that led to the declaration of rape as a war crime in Vienna in 1994. It was such an exercise that led to the Thai government proclama-tion of laws requiring brothel owners to insist upon condom use by the clients of sex workers. Similar successes have been recorded in Australia where sex work has been deregulated or in the Philippines and former Hong Kong where a convention on HIV and the workplace has been endorsed by the legislature. In South Africa, the constitutional rights of homosexuals have been upheld. This has been possible because the voices of men and women have been able to break out of the silence that has been enshrouding the intriguing area of sex and sexuality.

And as hope is rekindled, the issue of better access to curative and palliative medicines will need to be confronted. Very recently the leading US daily, *The New York Times,* carried the headline, 'Pain Relief Underused for Poor – Study Says'. The news item highlighted how a study conducted recently by the International Narcotics Control Board revealed a severe shortage of morphine and other pain killers in poor countries. The 10 largest consumer countries accounted for as much as 80 per cent of the analgesic morphine consumption of the world. We will need to tilt this balance because 90 per cent of HIV infections are occurring in countries that are resource poor and consume a small fraction of the world's resources. People living with HIV/AIDS need to live and die with dignity through continued access to at least the basic medicines required to treat opportunistic infections – ORT packets, drying powders, bandages, pain killers etc. In addition cheap antibiotics need to be made available to women and men to treat STDs such as chlamydia and gonorrhoea which make them more susceptible to HIV/AIDS. Studies suggest that treating such conditions with cheap antibiotics can cut new HIV infections by as much as 40 per cent.

I do not feel comfortable taking the discussion to a more compelling and aggressive advocacy of access to AZT, or to vaginal microbicides or, for that matter, even to the rather costly female condom. For if I do, I would be moving onto an unreal though desirable plane. The cost of triple drug therapy amounts to $500 per person per year even after the recent reductions negotiated with the drug companies. The prospects of resources being available to treat each case of HIV/AIDS per year in the less advantaged part of the globe is dismal.

Table 6

Botswana	$14.27
Kenya	$13.43
Malawi	$8.94
Mozambique	$2.40
Namibia	$8.00
Rwanda	$27.63
Zambia	$8.07
Zimbabwe	$9.32

Source: Jeffrey Bartholet, Newsweek, 17 January 2000

As flickering flames are rekindled, needs assessments of orphans and care-givers in the worst affected countries are being undertaken. Emotional and practical support is being promised to those who come out with their HIV status and a spirit of social inclusion is being fostered. Efforts have begun to empower women to be able to negotiate safe sex with their partners. Adolescents are being helped to make informed sexual choices. Data collection processes and procedures on the epidemic are being revised. In some of the worst affected countries AIDS is being declared as a national disaster, backed by the establishment of Crisis Management Committees. The mandate of these committees is to crest the epidemic at a lower level than projected.

Some options seem to be closing. Believing that HIV/AIDS is some-one else's problem is no longer an option. Believing that HIV/AIDS is just another disease is no longer an option. The only options are acknowledg-ing that HIV/AIDS is a crime against society; acknowledging that the orphans of the new generation have a boundless horizon before them; acknowledging that the walls of sexual oppression need to be scaled, if not torn down; acknowledging that the way ahead needs to be built on expanded partnerships compatible with national priorities, sensitive to local contexts, driven by innovation and above all ethically unassailable. Only then will we be able to translate human tragedy to human hope.

Glossary

Babu – permanent or long term clients of sex workers

Chokri – young girl

Dowry – price paid by the girl's father to her in-laws at the time of marriage

Didi – elder sister

Gishiri – a salt cut

Jekem – a material fermented from human faeces

Malkins – female brothel owners

Mukhiya – chief

Panchayat – local self government

Shambha – farmland

Tali – wedding thread

Valliakappu – a ritual performed during pregnancy

Bibliography

Aggleton, P. and Bertozzi, S.M., 'Socio-economic Impact of HIV/AIDS on Households, Chiangmai'. Geneva: World Health Organisation, 1997.

All India Institute of Hygiene and Public Health, 'A Dream, a Pledge, a Fulfilment'. Annual Report. New Delhi: India, 1992–97.

Alpha, Boubacar Diallo, 'A Tora Moussa Kela La'. New York: UNDP, 1996.

Bloom, D. and Lyons, J., The Economic Implications of AIDS in Asia. New Delhi: HIV/AIDS Regional Project. UNDP, 1993.

De, Bruyn M., 'Women and AIDS in Developing Countries'. Social Science and Medicine, No. 34(3), 1992.

Durbar Mahila Samanwaya Committee, The Fallen Learn to Rise. Sonagachi, Calcutta: India, 1998.

Farmer, P., Connor, M., and Simmons, J., Women, Poverty and AIDS. Maine, USA: Common Courage Press, 1996.

Hunter, S., Children on the brink. US Agency for International Development. Washington DC, 2000.

Nath, Madhu Bala, She Can Cope. New Delhi: National AIDS Control Programme, India, 1997.

Panos, AIDS and Men. London: Zed Press, 1999.

Ray, Sunanda, Women and AIDS. Geneva: World Health Organisation, 1992.

Schoofs, Mark, 'AIDS – The Agony of Africa'. New York: 2000 W Publishing Corporation, November 1999.

Solomon, S. and Pachauri, R., Whispers from Within. Chennai, New Delhi: YRG Centre for AIDS Research and Education, 1997.

Topouzis, D., 'The Implications of HIV/AIDS for Rural Development Policy and Programming'. New York: UNDP, 1998.

Topouzis, D. and Hemrich, *The Socioeconomic Impact of HIV/AIDS on Rural Families in Uganda: Emphasis on Youth*. New York: UNDP, 1992.

Tuju, Raphael. *Understanding the Challenge – AIDS in Kenya*, 1995.

Whelan, D. and Rao, G., 'Taking Stock on Gender and HIV/AIDS'. Washington DC: International Centre for Research on Women, 1997.

World Health Organisation, *Images of the Epidemic*. Geneva: WHO, 1993.

UNAIDS, 'AIDS 5 Years Since ICPD – Emerging Issues and Challenges for Women, Young People and Infants'. Discussion document. Geneva: UNAIDS, 1998.

UNAIDS/WHO (United Nations Programme on HIV/AIDS/World Health Organisation), UNAIDS Fact Sheet. Geneva, 1996, 1997, 1998, 1999.

United Nations Development Programme, *Human Development Report*. New York: Oxford University Press, 1999.

SOCIAL SCIENCE LIBRARY

Oxford University Library Services
Manor Road
Oxford OX1 3UQ
Tel: (2)71093 (enquiries and renewals)
http://www.ssl.ox.ac.uk

This is a NORMAL LOAN item.

We will email you a reminder before this item is due.

Please see http://www.ssl.ox.ac.uk/lending.html
for details on:

- loan policies; these are also displayed on the notice boards and in our library guide.

- how to check when your books are due back.

- how to renew your books, including information on the maximum number of renewals. Items may be renewed if not reserved by another reader. Items must be renewed before the library closes on the due date.

- level of fines; fines are charged on overdue books.

Please note that this item may be recalled during Term.

Barcode at front